TABLE OF

Contents

RECIPES
Photo Index

MIMOSA
Munchies

34 Banana Dollar Pancake Towers

36 Pumpkin Waffle Strips

38 Spicy Hash Stackers

40 Herbed Biscuits with Bacon Jam

42 Sweet Potato Breakfast Sandwiches

44 Strawberry-Banana Pancakes with Strawberry Syrup

46 Ham and Egg Cups

48 Prosciutto-Wrapped Melon

50 Avocado-Deviled Eggs

52 Spicy Ranchero Egg Salad

52 Dill Egg Salad

54 Sausage Mini Quiches

56 Red, White, and Blueberry Skewers

APPETIZERS

60
Teriyaki Beef Skewers

62
Scallop Bacon Sandwiches

64
General Tao's Chicken Wings

66
Chorizo-Stuffed Peppers

68
Jalapeño Bacon Poppers

70
Fajita Skewers

72
Smoky Bacon-Wrapped Shrimp

74
Yellow Curry Skewers

76
Mini Dogs with Cranberry Chili Sauce

78
Philly Steak Roll-Ups

80
Sweet Potato Slices with Avocado Ranch

82
Bacon Brussels Sprout Skewers

84
BLT Cucumber Rounds

86
Bacon-Wrapped Water Chestnuts

88
Spicy Sausage-Stuffed Mushrooms

90
Teriyaki Meatball Pineapple Skewers

92
Smoked Salmon Bites with Lemon-Dill Aioli

94
Shrimp Cocktail

96
Bruschetta-Stuffed Mushrooms

98
Chorizo Spanish "Tortilla"

100
Crab Salad Cucumber Rolls

102
Marinated Mushrooms

104
Antipasto Roll-Ups

106
Pesto-Stuffed Tomatoes

SMALL PLATES

110
Spaghetti Squash
Fritters with Meatballs

112
Eggplant Pizzas

114
Crab Cakes with
Wasabi-Avocado Sauce

116
Taco Sliders with
Chipotle Aioli

118
Barbecue Bacon
Mini Meatloaves

120
Aunt Esther's
Famous Ribs

122
Lemon Chicken
Skewers with
Almond Satay Sauce

124
Asian Chicken
Lettuce Cups with
Grape "Hoisin" Sauce

126
Lamb Dolmas
with Egg-Lemon
Sauce

128
Eggplant Sausage
Sliders

130
Lamb Lollipops
with Apricot-
Balsamic Glaze

132
Paleo Sushi

134
Crab-Stuffed
Mini Portobello
Mushrooms

136
Curry Chicken
Patties with
Cilantro-Lime Aioli

138
Tuna Tartare Towers

140
Mango Gazpacho
and Blackened
Shrimp

142
Seared Tuna with
Wasabi Slaw

144
Shrimp and
Scallop Ceviche

146
Garlic Clams

148
Pork Saucers with
Pear Compote

150
Parsnip Cakes with
Prosciutto

PUB GRUB

154
Bacon Mushroom Sliders

156
Beefed-Up Chili

158
Clam and Cauliflower Chowder

160
Coconut Shrimp with Mango-Habañero Dipping Sauce

162
Jalapeño and Bacon Chicken Rolls

164
Orange-Chipotle Barbecue Chicken Wings

166
Bacon-Wrapped Chicken

168
Chicken Fingers with Honey Mustard Sauce

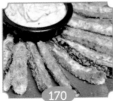

170
Zucchini Fries with Sweet Onion Dip

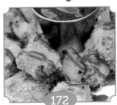

172
Buffalo Chicken Bites

174
Pulled Pork with Barbecue Sauce

176
Popcorn Shrimp with Tartar Sauce

178
Pizza Soup

180
California Burrito Bowl

SALOON SIDES

184 Parsnip Chips

186 Onion Rings

188 Herbed Butternut Squash Fries

190 Spicy Sweet Potato Fries

192 Chipotle-Roasted Potato Salad

194 Prosciutto-Wrapped Asparagus with Balsamic Glaze

196 Orange Hummus

198 Guacamole and Plantain Chips

200 Broccoli Slaw with Sweet Poppy Seed Dressing

202 Chicken Caesar Endive Boats

204 Apple Chips

206 Curried Cauliflower with Masala Dip

208 Spinach Dip and Jicama Chips

210 Zucchini Fritters with Lemon-Dill Aioli

212 Chinese Chicken Salad

214 Mini Wedge Salads with Avocado Ranch Dressing

216 Butternut Squash Soufflés

218 Herb-Infused Grilled Artichokes

220 Butternut Squash Rounds with Arugula Salad

222 Coleslaw with Creamy Dressing

SWEET TREATS

226 Apple Nachos

228 Cookie Dough Bonbons

230 Apple Torte

232 Almond Butter Bars

234 Pecan Pie Bars

236 Chocolate Crêpes with Strawberries and Chocolate Sauce

238 Almond Coconut Ice Cream Sundaes

240 Strawberry-Lime Sorbet

242 Coconut-Baked Bananas and Vanilla Ice Cream

244 Million-Dollar Chocolate Fondue

DELECTABLE DRINKS

248
•Blueberry Mint Juleps
•Light Sea Breezes
•Pom-y Tequila Sunrises

250
•Cucumber Mojitos
•Strawberry Daiquiris
•Piña Coladas

252
•Creamy Coffee
•Peppermint Chocolate Dream
•Spiked Apple Cider

254
•Spicy Jalapeño Margaritas
•Mango Margaritas

256
•Classic Margaritas
•Creamy Avocado-rita

258
•Peach Bellinis
•Pear Bellinis

260
•Tropical Pineapple Sangria
•Perfect Pear Sangria

262
•Classy Cosmos
•Dirty Martinis

264
•Pumpkin Pie Martinis
•Watermelon Slushi-tinis

ROBB'S FOREWORD

Howdy!

If you are perusing a book whose title has the word *Paleo* in it, you likely fall into one of two camps of people who are very interested in this way of eating:

1 You have serious health concerns or weight to lose, and you have heard that the Paleo diet is effective for a host of problems ranging from obesity to autoimmune disease.

2 You consider yourself a hard-charging athlete, and you have heard that the Paleo diet can help you perform better and recover faster than the standard diet most athletes eat.

You might not fall into either of these camps. Perhaps you're just a foodie with a bit of Paleo curiosity. Or maybe you're looking for new Paleo-friendly recipes and drink options that won't send your friends running for the door during social gatherings. The bottom line is that we all tend to have the same sorts of needs: Once we are healthy, looking and feeling good, we are ready to have some fun, kick up our heels, and enjoy some delicious yet healthy foods and drinks that satisfy our cravings.

I discovered this Paleo concept nearly 15 years ago as a very sick research biochemist. I had digestive issues (ulcerative colitis), high blood pressure, and a number of other nasty problems that you would not expect a (then) 28-year-old science geek and former California state powerlifting champion to be suffering from.

My grain-based vegan diet was just not working well for me. I had a laundry list of doctors and other healthcare providers trying to keep the wheels on my wagon, but I was a mess—such a mess that the notion of eating like a caveman was not at all off-putting. It was, in fact, a lifesaver. Paleo eating resolved my digestive issues, dropped my blood pressure, and restored my health.

Once I'd regained my health, I was pretty happy (and feeling much better, too). However, it took me a while to figure out that now that I was not in danger of dying, it was time to starting living and thriving. It was time to start enjoying the Paleo-adapted foods and drinks that I had been avoiding.

The simple fact is that most people enjoy eating finger foods and having a drink from time to time. I mean, who doesn't enjoy chicken wings, desserts, and cocktails? The problem is this: Abiding by the Paleo Diet is often difficult, especially in social situations. Enter *Paleo Happy Hour.*

Kelly Milton has done a great job of making otherwise unhealthy foods and drinks work for Paleo-conscious individuals. Need to cater an event or throw a party? Well, you're going to need some healthy finger foods, desserts, and drinks. And Kelly has you covered. She's provided the least-of-all-evil food and drink options without compromising your health or your taste buds—or turning off your non-Paleo-eating guests.

Now, I know what you're thinking: How exactly does alcohol factor into the Paleo diet?

As a coach and speaker, I get this question a lot. People are legitimately concerned that they will never be able to enjoy an alcoholic beverage or eat cake again. It's important to realize that binge drinking and eating a ton of gluten-free desserts and finger foods are not what you would consider Paleo. In fact, this kind of overindulgence will derail your health and have less-than-ideal physiological consequences. However, it's unrealistic to assume that you're never going to eat desserts or finger foods or enjoy the occasional drink. Just keep things in moderation, and do your best not to derail your health. To help folks out, I developed what you might call...

ROBB'S RULES OF DRINKING:

- Drink enough to optimize your sex life, but not so much that you impact performance.

- If possible, stick with clear booze, wine, and mixed drinks like the famous NorCal Margarita—100-percent agave tequila, plenty of fresh-squeezed lime juice, and soda water.

- To avoid compromising sleep, start drinking earlier in the day (that's right, folks, daytime drinking is best), and then sober up with a fatty meal.

Over time I figured out that a little booze is just fine with my system, as long as I avoid sugary drinks and beer containing gluten. If you can't handle alcohol due to an autoimmune issue or for some other reason, the solution is simple—avoid it, or make a mocktail (a cocktail without the alcohol).

I also discovered that it's nice to throw a party and serve food that is both familiar and healthy. I put a few of those pieces together myself, but Kelly Milton has brought it all together with her book *Paleo Happy Hour.* Who would have thought that you could throw a pub-style party and make foods from Paleo ingredients, while washing it back with some tasty drinks?

Take some time to read Kelly's introduction so that you can get an idea of how social eating and drinking can fit into your Paleo lifestyle. Then get in the kitchen and start mixing some drinks and cooking up these delicious recipes.

ACKNOWLEDGMENTS

First, I must thank my parents, John and Mary Milton. They have inspired me and supported me in every way imaginable. My love for cooking stems from my childhood experiences with food. Homemade meals were important. Every single night, we gathered around the dinner table to share food and conversation. My dad praised my first attempts at plating when I arranged vegetables into a smiley face on a salad. My mother experimented with fresh, gourmet recipes, exposing us to literally hundreds of diverse dishes. My passion for healthy cooking, creativity, imagination, and work ethic are a reflection of my parents' values. They have encouraged me in all of my endeavors. When I said I was eating Paleo, they jumped on board and catered family gatherings to my new diet. When I said I needed help editing this book, they provided countless hours of assistance. A thank you doesn't begin to express the gratitude I feel.

To my boyfriend, Robert Strazzarino, thank you. You encouraged me to start this journey at NorCal Strength and Conditioning Gym. Your belief that good nutrition is the foundation of good health has inspired me to embrace and maintain a Paleo lifestyle. When we discussed the possible challenges that we would face if I chose to write this book, you offered your unconditional support. You willingly volunteered to taste recipes and ate appetizers for dinner for six months without complaining. The process of testing recipes and preparing for photo shoots produced endless piles of dirty dishes, pots, pans, and staging props. You willingly helped with the monumental task of dishwashing without complaining. When I was too exhausted to lift another finger and felt overwhelmed by the workload, you offered me countless hours of emotional support as well. You were patient when our relationship was put on the back burner for this cookbook. You lent your technological expertise to the project by revamping my blog, designing my ergonomic workstation, and managing all of my IT needs. Thank you for being an amazing boyfriend throughout this adventure.

To my friends, you have also played a big role in this project. You were my cheerleaders! You showed an interest in my book, checked in to see how I was doing, taste-tested my recipes, and complimented my cooking skills. Despite the fact that this cookbook has dominated our conversations in recent months, you never seemed to tire of it. Julie Arndt and Shea McMullen, you made me dinner when cooking was the last thing I wanted to do and tasted foods you might have otherwise avoided. Erin West, you offered to keep me company during the many hours of food prep before a photo shoot. Stephanie Strazzarino, my boyfriend's sister, you provided another Paleo palate and lightened some of my hours in the kitchen with your sense of humor.

To my coworkers and good friends, Stephanie Valdes, Holly Sorensen, Lori Escobar, and Lauren Gras, you lent friendly ears to my venting pretty much every Monday through Friday. To Rachel and Brad Armstrong, you reminded me that my recipes could be tasty even to a picky two-year-old and showed me how well Paleo works for both of you.

To my other friends, Carissa Fanucchi-Christie, Kandi Manhart, Carly Lemmo, Becca Schmidt, and Cyndee Mendonca, you have been patient during this busy time in my life. It's comforting to know that we will pick up right where we left off. Thank you for your loving support throughout this project.

Last but not least, thank you to my NorCal Strength and Conditioning family. Robb Wolf, Nicki Violetti, Shawn Gower, Chrissy Gower, Katie DeLuca, Glen Cordoza, Matt Brown, Christina Curtiz, Sarah Fragoso, and John Fragoso, you have been such fun and healthy role models for what it means to live Paleo. Our shared drinks and meals helped inspire me to write this book. Chrissy, thank you so much for encouraging me and sharing your own book writing expertise. Glen, thank you for providing me with the opportunity to turn my vision for a cookbook into reality. Everyone at the gym, your conversations, laughter, and passion for fitness have continuously fueled my pursuit of Paleo.

MY PALEO
Journey

I first heard about Paleo when I started attending NorCal Strength and Conditioning Gym in Chico, California. In the On Ramp Class, the trainers discussed the benefits of a Paleo lifestyle. It was hard to wrap my head around the idea of eliminating foods that I had been enjoying my entire life. As a calorie-counting, carb-loving, sweet tooth kind of girl, I relied on portion control for weight management. However, I soon learned that a low number on the scale is not actually a measurement of good health. Robb Wolf's book, *The Paleo Solution*, helped me understand the health advantages of a grain-free, dairy-free, no-sugar-added diet. With my newfound knowledge, I began to transition to a Paleo lifestyle.

Despite my efforts to eat Paleo, I found myself frequently giving in to temptations at work and on the weekends. To truly explore this new way of eating, I needed to stop cheating. I decided to start my own 30-day challenge. Sarah Fragoso mentioned on her blog, *Everyday Paleo*, that blogging helped hold her accountable. Inspired, I created my own blog, *Paleo Girl's Kitchen*, to share my 30-day journey. Starting this journey in December posed many challenges given the seemingly endless holiday parties, office treats, and homemade sweets. Even though it was a struggle, I maintained my blog and my commitment to 30 days of strict Paleo.

By the end of my 30 days, I had experienced amazing results. I had dropped 10 pounds, and my strong cravings for non-Paleo foods had practically vanished. After eliminating processed sugar from my diet, natural sugar tasted so much sweeter! An apple became a satisfying dessert. My restless nights of insomnia were replaced with full nights of sound sleep. The bloating and gas that I had commonly experienced were, gratefully, no longer an issue. Creating Paleo versions of my favorite recipes became an exciting process. The Paleo diet had proved very rewarding.

Immediately following my 30-day challenge, the gym held a Paleo challenge. Wanting to maintain my new eating habits, I joined the challenge for extra support.

When the Paleo challenges were over, my food focus began to blur. I became more aware of the temptations that still surrounded me. While I loved my improved physical appearance and health, I definitely missed some non-Paleo foods.

15

Social situations made it hard to stick with the plan. From bar nights to dinner parties, my weekends were filled with environments that seemed impossible to navigate. Some Paleo followers talk about the 80/20 rule: 80 percent of the time you eat strict Paleo, and 20 percent of the time you don't. With this equation in place, I watched as the pounds crept back on. Slowly, 20 percent non-Paleo turned into 25 percent and more. It was a slippery slope into my old unhealthy eating habits.

I needed to find a way to make Paleo fit my lifestyle 100 percent of the time. In an effort to merge my social life and the Paleo diet, I decided to host a Valentine's Day party. I served only Paleo food, and to my surprise, everyone ate it! Some guests even voiced their appreciation of the healthier spread.

Next, I took on the task of catering the holiday party at NorCal Strength and Conditioning Gym. Everyone devoured the elaborate buffet of Paleo-friendly appetizers and desserts. Gym members approached me asking for the recipes for dishes ranging from chicken with almond satay sauce to sausage-stuffed mushrooms and chocolate-covered strawberries. This experience encouraged

me to keep blogging and sharing my recipes. I had begun to break down the wall between healthy eating and socializing.

On a trip to Thailand, I visited with Katie DeLuca, a trainer from my gym, and Glen Cordoza, an author. They are both in amazing shape and eat strict Paleo. While we sipped drinks at the pool, they acknowledged how challenging it is to stay Paleo in social situations. We all agreed that there wasn't a good resource for Paleo partiers. Having enjoyed my Paleo recipes in the past, Glen encouraged me to write a book containing food and drink recipes and general tips. As I left my adventures in Thailand behind, I returned home to begin yet another adventure—writing this book.

I truly hope that you find this book to be a useful tool in your journey toward achieving good health. I encourage you to use the advice provided if you struggle to stay on track in social situations. It isn't easy to make healthy food choices when drinking impairs your judgment or when your friends beg you to indulge in late-night pizza. But the tips on the following pages can help you navigate the SAD (Standard American Diet) world we live in. These recipes can impress your guests or add variety to your weekly meals. Indulge in some of these drinks on special occasions, taking comfort in knowing that they don't contain tons of sugar, corn syrup, or artificial flavors. Take this diet with a grain of (sea) salt, and allow yourself the freedom to enjoy a cocktail or dessert without going rogue.

INTRODUCTION

It's Friday! You worked all week, made healthy meals, hit the gym, ran errands, did laundry, walked the dog, and cleaned the house. Now it's time for a reward—happy hour. So do you ditch the diet and savor a syrupy-sweet mudslide while popping pieces of fried calamari and gossiping with friends? Or do you go home and slump into your couch with a bowl of salad? You no longer have to choose! Let this book help you meld the worlds of gluttonous gatherings and Paleo perfection.

While you might be tempted to leaf quickly past the next few pages to get to the drool-worthy food, I challenge you to take the time to read this information. It will help you address the complex challenges posed by committing to a Paleo lifestyle while maintaining an active social life.

You can examine the pros and cons of making alcohol part of your plan. If you choose to include it, my alcohol and mixer charts demonstrate how alcohol can comply with Paleo principles. You will also learn valuable strategies for drinking and eating at restaurants, bars, and parties. When you're on your way to a party, be sure to review the 10 Paleo Party Rules, which will guarantee your success.

Armed with these tips, you can explore my tantalizing food recipes. While some of these dishes involve a lot of preparation, the results are delicious and worth it! Don't limit the use of the recipes to entertaining. Try one of the appetizers as a weekday lunch, or pair a small plate with a salad for a quick dinner.

You may find recipes that include ingredients that fall into the "Paleo gray area." If you prefer to maintain a strict Paleo diet, avoid these recipes or make ingredient substitutions as you see fit.

The drink recipes are just a few of my favorites. Many can be made into tasty mocktails without alcohol. The sample party menus at the end of the book show you how to pair these drinks with food. There are limitless drink possibilities, so use my alcohol and mixer charts to come up with your own healthy combinations.

As a host, I pride myself on throwing the kinds of gatherings where guests compliment the food, savor the drinks, and leave asking for the recipes. I take comfort in knowing that what I've served hasn't compromised my health or theirs. Whether you are ready to host your own Paleo party or just want to have a crowd-pleasing dish to take to events, let this book be your guide to freeing your inner social butterfly without sabotaging your health.

ALCOHOL
&
PALEO

IN DEFENSE OF DRINKING

A question that many people ask when starting their Paleo journey is, "Where does alcohol fit in?" This section explores the advantages and disadvantages of including alcohol in your life. If your primary Paleo goal is weight loss or body composition changes, alcohol can impede your progress, but it doesn't have to derail your efforts. In fact, drinking in moderation offers some health benefits.

Alcohol can act as a blood thinner, which can improve your vascular health. It also contains antioxidants (especially red wine), which can decrease your risk of cancer and reduce the signs of aging. Moderate drinking has even been linked to lower rates of heart disease, type 2 diabetes, and stroke. It can even lead to a longer life! So eliminating alcohol altogether isn't necessary.

Drinking can also reduce stress. As soon as I have had my first few sips of wine, I can feel myself begin to relax. Why is relaxation so important? Stress can lead to weight gain and premature aging. Many people suffer from emotional overeating, which can be triggered by stress as well. Stress can even elevate cortisol levels that take away from other bodily functions, like immunity and digestion. A drink is just one way you can help relieve stress.

Drinking plays a role in many social situations. Some people find that having a drink or two relieves their anxiety about socializing, especially when meeting new people or when dancing is involved. Alcohol is often served at events, and not partaking can be isolating. You don't want your diet to make you feel like you can't be social or fit in. By having a drink in these situations, you allow alcohol to be a part of your Paleo lifestyle, which can make it easier to maintain.

So don't feel guilty turning to a glass of red wine for relaxation after a stressful day and enjoying the benefits of the antioxidants. As long as you drink in moderation, there is no need to worry. Raise your glass, and say "Cheers" to Paleo-friendly partying.

DRINKERS BEWARE!

While drinking in moderation has some benefits, there are many health risks as well. Drinking to excess can have a negative effect on your overall health, and it leads to weight and fat gain. So before you install a kegerator of your favorite hard cider, there are a few things to consider.

Alcohol can increase your likelihood of getting certain kinds of cancer. Overconsumption of alcohol can damage your liver and negatively affect the quality of your sleep. It's an addictive, mind-altering substance, so regular consumption or overconsumption can lead to alcoholism. Take these risks into consideration before deciding whether drinking alcohol is right for you.

Alcohol can also negatively impact your body composition. Most drinks contain carbohydrates, which can lead to fat storage. Alcohol spikes your blood sugar. When your blood sugar levels crash the next day or even later that night, you will feel hungry and experience cravings that can lead to overeating.

Drinking also impairs your judgment. The pizza you would normally avoid might be scarfed down without hesitation after drinking. So use caution when you decide to drink, particularly if improved body composition is your goal.

MOCKTAILS AND HYDRATION

If you're not a drinker or you want to drink in moderation, mocktails are a great substitute. Drinking a mocktail allows you to enjoy the flavor of a cocktail while avoiding the alcohol. I recommend picking a stirred or muddled drink, such as a sea breeze or mojito. Avoid virgin blended drinks, because they separate and melt without the alcohol. Also, if you find yourself drinking out of peer pressure, mocktails are the perfect cover. You can appear as if you are drinking, so no one will question you. Sometimes just having a glass in hand can make you feel more comfortable at an event where everyone else is holding a drink.

Even if you are drinking alcohol, try alternating an alcoholic beverage with a mocktail to slow your consumption. Drinking alcoholic beverages can lead to dehydration, which can cause many symptoms of a hangover, such as fatigue and headache. Mocktails can help you rehydrate, or you can alternate a glass of water between drinks for an even healthier option.

PALEO
Alcohol Guide

Most people would say that alcohol is not Paleo—it isn't healthy, and cavemen didn't drink it. This may be true, but there are people who eat a Paleo diet who want to include alcohol. This alcohol guide is not meant for people who are *strict* Paleo or who are working hard toward leaning out. This section is for people looking for alcoholic beverage choices that are Paleo friendly.

This guide is based on Paleo principles that are applicable to alcohol and mixers: grain-free, dairy-free, and no added refined sugars. Use it to help you navigate your drinking choices or create your own combinations.

BEST CHOICES:

(these are not derived from grains and contain no added refined sugar):

Tequila (from the agave plant)

Rum (from sugarcane)

Potato vodka (from potatoes)

GOOD CHOICES:

(these are not derived from grains but have a higher carbohydrate content):

Wine

Gluten-free beer

Champagne

ACCEPTABLE CHOICES:

(these are derived from grains but are gluten-free):

Gin

Vodka*

Whiskey*

Scotch*

Hard cider**

NOT-SO-GREAT CHOICES:

(these are gluten-free but high in sugar):

Liqueurs

Dessert wines (port)

ALCOHOL TO AVOID:

(these may contain gluten, dairy, or added sugar):

Beer

Wine coolers

Premixed cocktails (margarita, mudslide, piña colada, cosmopolitan)

* According to the Canadian Celiac Association, these distilled alcoholic beverages do not contain prolamins (gluten proteins).

** Research your cider choice, as some varieties contain gluten or are higher in carbohydrates and sugar.

MIXERS
Guide

Often, the alcohol isn't the worst part of a drink; the mixer is the worst part. Many popular mixers are filled with sugar, sodium, and artificial additives. Whenever possible, use freshly squeezed juices or blended whole fruits that are in season. You can also use vegetable mixers, as in a bloody Mary or a cucumber mojito.

There are many benefits to mixing. Using a mixer adds volume to your drinks, dilutes the alcohol, and potentially slows your consumption. You also get additional vitamins from the fresh fruits and vegetables. Mixers allow you to make drinks that are delicious, enjoyable, and nutritious.

On the other hand, mixers raise the carbohydrate content of drinks, so when you know that you will be indulging in a mixed drink or two, eat fewer carbs throughout the day. Then mix away guilt-free!

BEST CHOICES:

Freshly squeezed juice (lime, lemon, orange)

Blended or muddled whole fruit (berries, pineapple, mangoes)

Blended or juiced vegetables (carrots, celery, cucumbers, tomatoes)

Club soda

ACCEPTABLE CHOICES:

100% whole fruit juice (not from concentrate)

Coconut milk

Coconut water

Honey (as a sweetener)

MIXERS TO AVOID:

Soda (regular and diet)

Fruit juice with added sugar

Grenadine and other flavored syrups

Premade mixers (margarita, mudslide, piña colada, cosmopolitan)

PALEO
Party tips

While this book prepares you to party Paleo style at home, the world beyond your front door poses different challenges with more temptations, tremendous pressures, and fewer healthy choices. From bars to house parties, each situation comes with its own set of difficulties. This section provides tips for coping with different situations.

On the Town
PALEO-STYLE DRINKS

Bars are a fun place to celebrate birthdays, spend happy hour with coworkers, or dance the night away. There are fewer Paleo-friendly options at bars, however. Here is a drinking chart for bars:

BEST CHOICES

Wine

Gluten-free beer

Dirty martini

Champagne

Tequila with soda water and lime wedges

GOOD CHOICES

Vodka cranberry or screwdriver (ask the bartender to substitute soda water for half the juice to lower the sugar content)

Cosmopolitan (ask the bartender to hold the Cointreau/orange liquor)

Mojito (ask them to go light on the simple syrup)

Hard cider

BAD CHOICES

Beer

Margarita

Specialty sweet drinks (piña colada, daiquiri, Long Island iced tea, rum and Coke)

These choices are "Best" for one reason: You can order them as is. If the bar is crowded or loud, you don't want to have to explain a special drink request to the bartender.

These are all healthy choices, but you need to trust that the bartender will be accommodating. Some restaurants use sugar mixers to make mojitos, so it's best to watch the bartender make your drink if you can.

Beer contains gluten, and the other drinks are very high in sugar. They may also contain dairy, corn syrup, food coloring, and artificial flavors.

FOOD

Now that you are prepared to make healthy drink choices, let's talk about food. For favorable bar food choices, look for something with meat or seafood. Many happy hour menus offer sliders (minus the buns), shrimp cocktail, seared ahi tuna, or blackened prawns. If you are at a place with a full menu, don't be afraid to ask to order from it. Then you can potentially get a nice side salad, soup, or entrée that is Paleo. If you know in advance that you're going out, check online for a menu so that you can look for Paleo options. If there are none, try to grab a quick bite before you go, or pack some trail mix in case you get hungry.

Making good food choices can be trickier if you become hungry while bar-hopping. A good choice is to locate a hamburger place and order a burger without the bun. If you spot a hot dog cart, don't feel guilty about downing a bunless dog. If these options aren't cutting it for you, and you want some greasy food to "absorb the alcohol," try to stay gluten-free with gluten-free pizza, corn tortilla tacos, or French fries as a last resort.

If you're headed to the bars for a special night, you can minimize the damage by downing a glass of water between alcoholic drinks. Also, get moving! Walk between bars, dance, or stand instead of sit. All of these activities will use up some of the extra carbohydrates you are consuming. Even though these activities are not a full-blown workout, they will help, especially if you limit yourself to one or two drinks.

HOUSE PARTIES

Parties and holidays can present problems when you are trying to stay committed to Paleo. You don't want to offend the host, so you could be a gracious guest by offering to bring food and drinks that are Paleo friendly. Also, consider eating before the event. Even if it's just beef jerky and a piece of fruit, you won't show up hungry to a party and make bad food choices as a result. By bringing your own food and drink or snacking beforehand, you should be able to attend and enjoy any gathering.

The pressure to people-please can be especially high at these events. You may be persuaded to indulge in wheat, dairy, and sugar-filled foods. Other guests may want the comfort of having you join them in unhealthy food choices. While giving in may ease their discomfort, you will undoubtedly feel worse. Sometimes, a host or guest might not understand why you won't eat the dessert they made "just for you." Try not to eat to please other people; eat for yourself.

If you do choose to eat a non-Paleo food, don't dwell on it. You're just adding guilt to your plate. However, you don't want a couple of chips to turn into a whole bag. Avoid using a small slip-up to justify a binge. Acknowledge how eating that food made you feel, and move on. Remember that parties are special occasions that are meant to be enjoyed, not add to your stress.

THE 10 PALEO PARTY RULES

1. FOOD FIRST.

Think about food before anything else. If you are going out drinking, eat a high-protein, low-carbohydrate dinner beforehand. You will get plenty of carbohydrates in your cocktails, so stick to protein and non-starchy vegetables for your pre-party meal. Pack a snack in your purse or car so that you won't be tempted to eat pizza at 2:00 a.m. If you're going to a dinner or house party, bring a healthy food option to share.

2. BE PREPARED.

Set goals for the night before you go out. Decide how many alcoholic beverages you plan to drink. Rehearse turning down unhealthy options like sugary mixed shots or chips and spinach dip. Being prepared will make it easier when the foreseeable challenges arise.

3. PRACTICE THE EVERY-OTHER RULE.

When you are at a party, it's comfortable to have a drink in hand, but no one said that it has to be alcoholic. Try having water or a mocktail between drinks. Doing so will keep you hydrated and reduce the number of alcoholic drinks you consume.

4. BE A GIVER.

Share your new favorite Paleo drink or food recipe. Don't hold out on your friends! Bring your own treats to a party, and let everyone enjoy a healthy option.

5. USE YOUR CARBS.

Ditch your drink, and get on the dance floor. Move while you are out partying. Dancing, walking between bars, or even standing (away from the buffet table) will help use up the carbs you consume.

6. DON'T PREACH; DO.

Look around. Are you at your CrossFit Christmas party? If not, it isn't appropriate to preach about Paleo. No one signed up for your seminar on nutrition, nor do you need to justify your food choices! If someone asks about your diet, give a short, heartfelt answer without passing judgment on the other person's lifestyle choices.

7. DRESS TO IMPRESS.

If you are living a healthy Paleo lifestyle, chances are you look good. So be sexy and know it! If you're a woman, wear a tight dress. If you're a guy, wear a tee that hugs those muscles. Not only do you get to show off the hot bod you have worked hard for, but you will also be less likely to indulge in late-night munchies. Nothing will keep you farther from the dessert table than form-fitting attire.

8. MOVE ON.

Whether you had two drinks or five, plus a late-night pizza, wake up the next day and get back on track. You will have extra carbs to burn, so plan to exercise. Don't fuel your hangover with greasy food. Pick up your Paleo diet right where you left off.

9. CREATE COMMUNITY.

Surround yourself with friends who share or support your health values. Plan social activities together that don't revolve around food or drinks. Participate in the Paleo online community for even more support.

10. DON'T STRESS! YOLO

(You only live once)! You need to enjoy life and the Paleo lifestyle. Beating yourself up and feeling bad every time you slip isn't any way to live. Paleo isn't a test. If you get upset about every little "cheat," you are more likely to quit altogether. If you are eating real food and living Paleo, you are ahead of the curve. So don't stress, and celebrate every small victory!

PALEO DRINKING
Cheat Sheet

BEST CHOICES:

TEQUILA
derived from a plant, gluten-free, sugar-free, low-carb.

POTATO VODKA
derived from potatoes, gluten-free, sugar-free, low-carb.

GOOD CHOICE:

VODKA-RUM-WHISKEY
derived from grain, wheat, corn but contain no gluten proteins sugar-free, low-carb.

SHAKEN

{or stirred} *EVEN MUDDLED*

-CLUB SODA
-ICE CUBES
-MUDDLED HERBS:
MINT, BASIL, GINGER
-FRESHLY SQUEEZED JUICE:
GRAPEFRUIT, LIME, ORANGE, LEMON
-COCONUT WATER
-COFFEE

HONEY {SPARINGLY}

Blended!
USE WHOLE FRUITS & VEGGIES!

THE ADDED FIBER FROM WHOLE FRUIT {VS. JUICE} WILL HELP STABILIZE YOUR BLOOD SUGAR AND FILL YOU UP!

VEGGIES: CUCUMBER, JALAPEÑO, AVOCADO
FROZEN OR FRESH FRUIT: STRAWBERRIES, BLUEBERRIES, ORANGES, LIMES, PEACHES, PEARS...AND MORE.
TROPICAL FRUITS {HIGHER IN SUGAR}: MANGOES, PINEAPPLE, BANANAS
GOOD-FAT MIXER: COCONUT MILK

READY-TO-DRINK OPTIONS
nutrition facts are approximate

4g Carbs
1g Sugar
5 oz.

WINE

12-24g Carbs
10g Sugar
12 oz.

HARD CIDER
make sure it's glute-free

1g Carbs
0g Sugar
4 oz.

CHAMPAGNE

12g Carbs
0g Sugar
12 oz.

GLUTEN-FREE BEER

WHY ARE SUGAR & CARBS IMPORTANT?

DRINKING SPIKES YOUR BLOOD SUGAR, WHICH YOU DON'T WANT. EVENTUALLY, WHEN YOUR BLOOD SUGAR CRASHES, IT CAN CAUSE CRAVINGS, IRRITABILITY AND HUNGER. ALSO, THE EXCESS CARBS AND SUGAR YOU CONSUME CAN BE STORED AS FAT.

THINGS TO AVOID

MIXED DRINKS
PIÑA COLADAS, MARGARITAS, MUDSLIDES, MARTINIS

WINE COOLERS
MIKE'S HARD LEMONADE, SMIRNOFF ICE, SPARKS

BEER
LIGHT BEER, DARK BEER, & EVERYTHING IN BETWEEN

LIQUEURS
COFFEE LIQUEUR, SCHNAPPS, FLAVORED VODKAS

MIXERS
SODA, DIET SODA, SYRUPS, ENERGY DRINKS

DRIVING!
DON'T DRINK AND DRIVE!
WALK {LIKE A CAVEMAN}

MIMOSA
Munchies

YUM

RISE
&
SHINE

MIMOSA MUNCHIES

INGREDIENTS:

2 bananas

4 eggs

½ teaspoon vanilla extract

1 tablespoon coconut flour

Avocado oil in an oil mister

Ghee

Maple syrup

SPECIAL TOOLS:

 BLENDER

• • •

MIMOSA MUNCHIES

• • •

BANANA DOLLAR
• • • PANCAKE TOWERS • • •

 SERVES: 4   PREP TIME: 3 MIN.   COOK TIME: 10 MIN.

These pancakes are tasty, easy, and guilt-free. Making them dollar-sized transforms them into an easy-to-eat finger food. They aren't quite as fluffy as traditional pancakes, but the texture is still enjoyable. Top these pancakes with fresh fruit tossed in a little honey or maple syrup.

1. In a blender, blend the bananas, eggs, vanilla extract, and coconut flour on high until smooth.

2. Mist a hot nonstick pan with avocado oil. Pour dollar-sized pancakes onto the pan, and cook for 2-3 minutes until they begin to bubble. Turn them over, and cook for an additional minute.

3. Serve the pancakes with ghee and maple syrup.

TIPS

To reheat these pancakes, pop them in a toaster oven. This will keep the texture consistent when reheating.

PUMPKIN WAFFLE

• • • STRIPS • • •

INGREDIENTS:

8 eggs

1 cup pumpkin purée

½ cup blanched almond flour

¼ cup coconut milk

2 tablespoons coconut flour, sifted

1 tablespoon honey

1 tablespoon pumpkin pie spice

1 teaspoon vanilla extract

½ teaspoon baking soda

Ghee

Maple syrup

SPECIAL TOOLS:

 WAFFLE IRON

• • •

MIMOSA MUNCHIES

36

 SERVES: 4   PREP TIME: 5 MIN.   COOK TIME: 16 MIN.

These pumpkin waffles are a great dish in the fall, and they are a good reason to purchase a waffle iron if you don't already own one. The familiar flavor of pumpkin pie spice adds sweetness. Cutting the waffles into strips makes them easy to share and to dip into maple syrup.

1. In a medium-sized bowl, whisk the eggs.

2. Stir in the pumpkin purée, almond flour, coconut milk, coconut flour, honey, pumpkin pie spice, vanilla extract, and baking soda, and mix until they are thoroughly combined.

3. Heat a waffle iron. Pour about one-quarter of the batter into the iron, and bake the waffle for 4 minutes. Repeat with the remaining batter.

4. Cut the waffles into ½-inch strips, and serve them with ghee and maple syrup.

TIPS

If you don't have a waffle iron, add ¼ cup more coconut milk to the batter, and prepare pancakes instead.

SPICY HASH
• • • STACKERS • • •

 SERVES: 4   PREP TIME: 15 MIN.   🔥 COOK TIME: 20 MIN.

These Spicy Hash Stackers are pleasing not only to the eye, but also to the stomach! Top these colorful spicy potato towers with a fried egg and a few browned sausage slices for extra protein. This flavorful dish is a perfect start to your day.

1. Peel the sweet potatoes, and cut them into ½-inch cubes. Place them in a bowl, cover it with plastic wrap, and microwave it on high for 4 minutes.

2. Spray a large frying pan with avocado oil. Over medium-high heat, sauté the onion, bell pepper, garlic, and jalapeño pepper for 2 minutes.

3. Add the sweet potatoes, olive oil, chili powder, cumin, sea salt, and cayenne pepper (if using) to the pan. Sauté on high for 7 minutes, stirring every couple of minutes.

4. In a separate frying pan over medium heat, cook the eggs. Use a spatula to prevent the eggs from spreading. After 2 minutes, turn the eggs and cook the other sides for 1-2 minutes, keeping the yolks slightly runny. Remove the eggs, and set them aside.

5. Thinly slice the chicken sausages into rounds. Using the pan in which you cooked the eggs, sauté the chicken sausages over medium-high heat until they are slightly browned.

6. To assemble the "hash stacks," press half of the sweet potato mixture into a 3-inch-round cookie cutter. Using the same cutter, trim the egg. Lay the egg on top of the sweet potatoes, and top it with a few slices of chicken sausage. Garnish with the chopped cilantro, if desired.

INGREDIENTS:

2 small sweet potatoes

Avocado oil in an oil mister

½ onion, chopped

½ red bell pepper, chopped

2 cloves garlic, minced

1 jalapeño pepper, seeded and minced

1 teaspoon olive oil

1½ teaspoons chili powder

1 teaspoon cumin

¼ teaspoon sea salt

¼ teaspoon cayenne pepper (optional)

4 large eggs

2 spicy chicken sausage links

1 tablespoon chopped cilantro (optional)

• • •

MIMOSA MUNCHIES

• • • •

38

INGREDIENTS:

BISCUITS

¾ cup blanched almond flour

½ cup coconut flour, sifted

1 teaspoon baking powder

½ teaspoon sea salt

1 teaspoon garlic powder

1 teaspoon onion powder

1 teaspoon oregano

1½ tablespoons coconut oil, refrigerated

7 egg whites

BACON JAM

1 pound bacon

¾ cup chopped yellow onion

2 cloves garlic, smashed

⅓ cup apple cider vinegar

½ cup brewed coffee

¼ cup maple syrup

1 tablespoon honey

SPECIAL TOOLS:

 STAND MIXER

 FOOD PROCESSOR

MIMOSA MUNCHIES

40

HERBED BISCUITS
• • • WITH BACON JAM • • •

 SERVES: 6   PREP TIME: 45 MIN.   COOK TIME: 25 MIN.

Bacon Jam is a Paleo dream. When you spread it on Herbed Biscuits, you create a delicious bite-sized dish that is easy to prepare and even easier to devour!

1. Preheat the oven to 400°F.

2. In a medium-sized bowl, stir together the almond flour, coconut flour, baking powder, sea salt, garlic powder, onion powder, and oregano.

3. Add the coconut oil to the mixture.

4. Using a stand mixer, beat the egg whites in a separate bowl for about 5 minutes or until they are foamy. Gently fold them into the flour mixture until combined.

5. Line a baking sheet with parchment paper. Use a cookie scoop or large spoon to drop 1½-inch spheres of the batter onto the parchment paper, making 12 bite-sized biscuits. Bake the biscuits for 13-15 minutes until the tops are golden brown.

6. Meanwhile, in a large skillet over medium-high heat, cook the bacon until it is browned, and set it aside.

7. Pour out most of the bacon grease, leaving a thin layer in the pan. Add the onion, garlic, apple cider vinegar, coffee, maple syrup, and honey to the skillet. Cook on high heat for 5 minutes, stirring occasionally. Remove the mixture, and place it in a food processor along with the bacon. Pulse the jam mixture until it reaches the desired consistency, and serve the jam with the warm rolls.

TIPS

If you prepare the Bacon Jam in advance, reheat it before serving to enhance both its appearance and its taste.

SWEET POTATO
• • • BREAKFAST SANDWICHES • • •

 **SERVES: 4**    **PREP TIME: 10 MIN.**   **COOK TIME: 45 MIN.**

INGREDIENTS:

1 wide sweet potato

1 tablespoon olive oil

½ teaspoon garlic powder

½ teaspoon onion powder

2 teaspoons dried rosemary

Dash sea salt

Avocado oil in an oil mister

8 eggs

8 slices Canadian bacon (or thick slices of ham)

We have all seen commercials for fast-food breakfast sandwiches. Even if their nutritional issues disgust you, admit it—they look pretty tasty. This recipe is a delicious Paleo rendition of the commercial version. Since the eggs and bacon are sandwiched between seasoned sweet potato slices, you won't miss the bread at all.

1. Preheat the oven to 425°F.

2. Slice the sweet potato into ¼-inch slices. In a large bowl, toss the potato slices with the olive oil, garlic powder, onion powder, rosemary, and sea salt.

3. Line a baking sheet with foil, and spray it with avocado oil. Spread the potato slices on the baking sheet in a single layer. Bake for 20-35 minutes, depending on the thickness of the sweet potato slices, turning them halfway through. When done, they should be cooked through and slightly browned.

4. Meanwhile, heat a large frying pan on medium-high heat. As the pan is heating, whisk 1 egg in a small bowl. Slowly pour the egg into the frying pan. As it begins to cook, push the edges inward to shape the egg into a circle that is approximately the same diameter as the sweet potato slices. Once the egg is sturdy enough to turn, flip it over, and cook it for 1 more minute. Repeat this procedure with the remaining eggs.

5. In a separate frying pan, cook the Canadian bacon on medium heat for 1 minute per side.

6. To assemble the sandwiches, start with 1 potato slice, top it with an egg and a slice of bacon, and finish it with an additional sweet potato slice. Serve hot.

TIPS

If you have a lot of hungry guests, serve these sandwiches open-faced. You will need to double the amount of eggs and bacon, however.

Consider purchasing an egg ring. They are inexpensive, simplify egg preparation, and improve the presentation.

Get creative by adding onions and bell peppers to the eggs. You can also add avocado to the sandwich or replace the Canadian bacon with traditional bacon. The possibilities are endless!

MIMOSA MUNCHIES

STRAWBERRY-BANANA PANCAKES

• • • WITH STRAWBERRY SYRUP • • •

 SERVES: 4   **PREP TIME: 5 MIN.**   **COOK TIME: 15 MIN.**

INGREDIENTS:

PANCAKES

5 eggs

1 ripe banana

5 strawberries, fresh or frozen

¼ cup blanched almond flour

1 teaspoon vanilla extract

Avocado oil in an oil mister

SYRUP

1½ cups frozen organic
   strawberries

¼ cup organic coconut sugar

These sweet pancakes fuse the flavors of bananas and strawberries. Add an extra burst of strawberry bliss with the homemade syrup.

1. In a blender or food processor, blend the eggs, banana, strawberries, almond flour, and vanilla extract until smooth.

2. Heat a large frying pan on medium-high heat, and spray it with avocado oil. Pour dollar-sized circles of batter into the pan. Cook for 2 minutes. Then turn the pancakes, and cook the other sides for 1 minute.

3. To make the syrup, defrost the strawberries in the microwave for about 1 minute.

4. In a blender on the high setting, blend the strawberries with any extra juice and the coconut sugar until smooth.

5. Transfer the syrup to a small saucepan, and heat it on the stovetop or in the microwave. Serve the warm syrup over the pancakes.

SPECIAL TOOLS:

  BLENDER OR FOOD PROCESSOR

• • •

MIMOSA MUNCHIES

• • •

44

TIPS

To reheat these pancakes, use a toaster oven. This will ensure that the pancakes maintain their great texture; they become soggy in the microwave.

HAM AND EGG

• • • CUPS • • •

 SERVES: 6   PREP TIME: 10 MIN.   COOK TIME: 20 MIN.

Part of the success of this dish is that it's an easy way to make eggs for a large number of people. The ham creates lovely little cups that are easy to pick up and eat, making this recipe perfect for a breakfast buffet.

1. Preheat the oven to 400°F.

2. In a large frying pan, melt the ghee over medium-high heat. Add the mushrooms and onion to the pan, and sauté them for 3-5 minutes or until tender. Set them aside.

3. Lightly coat a muffin tin with avocado oil. Line each portion with a piece of ham. Place a spoonful of the mushroom mixture in each ham cup, and crack an egg on top of each cup.

4. Bake the cups for 15-17 minutes or until the egg whites are completely cooked and the yolks are the consistency you prefer. Serve with freshly ground pepper.

INGREDIENTS:

1½ teaspoons ghee

6 mushrooms, finely chopped

½ cup finely chopped yellow onion

Avocado oil in an oil mister

12 thin slices ham

12 medium eggs

Freshly ground black pepper to taste

TIPS

Experiment with other ingredients in the sauté, such as chopped artichoke hearts, sausage, tomatoes, or green onion. If you're feeding a big crowd, each dozen could include a different combination of ingredients. Also, some guests may prefer scrambled eggs, so you can beat the eggs before pouring them into the ham cups.

• • •

MIMOSA MUNCHIES

• • •

46

PROSCIUTTO-WRAPPED

• • • MELON • • •

 SERVES: 4-6   PREP TIME: 15 MIN.

Weaving the prosciutto around the orange cantaloupe balls produces a presentation that will surely impress your guests. The combination of salty prosciutto and sweet melon will also delight their taste buds.

1. Halve the cantaloupe, and remove the seeds. With a large melon baller, scoop out the melon balls, and set them aside in a bowl.

2. Very carefully separate the prosciutto slices, and slice them in half lengthwise.

3. To assemble, thread one end of the prosciutto onto the end of a skewer. Add a melon ball to the skewer, and weave the prosciutto around the melon and back through the skewer. Move the prosciutto and the melon ball down the skewer, and repeat this process 2 more times. Serve immediately, or refrigerate until ready to eat.

INGREDIENTS:

1 cantaloupe (or other type of melon, such as honeydew, Crenshaw, or casaba)

1 package prosciutto

Small wooden skewers

• • •

MIMOSA MUNCHIES

48

TIPS

If you are in a time crunch, you can just slice the cantaloupe and serve it alongside the prosciutto.

AVOCADO-DEVILED
• • • EGGS • • •

INGREDIENTS:

12 eggs

1 avocado

4 tablespoons Paleo Mayonnaise (page 267)

1 tablespoon spicy brown mustard

2 teaspoons freshly squeezed lemon juice

½ teaspoon sea salt

½ teaspoon paprika or cayenne pepper

 SERVES: 6-10   PREP TIME: 15 MIN.   COOK TIME: 25 MIN.

This variation of a classic appetizer will please the pickiest eaters and be easy on your wallet. Adding avocado to the filling makes it extra creamy and colorful.

1. Place the eggs in a large pot, and cover them with 1 inch of water. Bring the water to a boil, and boil the eggs for 1 minute. Reduce the heat to low, and cook the eggs for an additional 20 minutes.

2. When the eggs are done, drain and rinse them under cold water. Peel them immediately, cut them in half, and separate the yolks from the whites. Set the egg whites aside.

3. In a food processor, combine the egg yolks, avocado, Paleo Mayonnaise, mustard, lemon juice, and sea salt. Spoon the mixture back into the egg whites, creating small mounds. You can also use a pastry bag to fill the eggs.

4. Place the deviled eggs on a serving platter, and sprinkle them with paprika or cayenne pepper. Serve immediately or refrigerate them.

SPECIAL TOOLS:

 FOOD PROCESSOR

• • •
MIMOSA MUNCHIES
• • •

50

▶ TIPS ◀

To save time the day of an event, boil and peel the eggs the night before.

To keep the avocado mixture from browning, store it in a container covered with plastic wrap. Press the plastic wrap down to completely cover the top of the avocado mixture so that air cannot penetrate. Before serving, stir the mixture and fill the eggs.

SPICY RANCHERO

• • • EGG SALAD • • •

 SERVES: 6   PREP TIME: 20 MIN.

The flavors of jalapeño, white onion, and spices add flair to this traditional recipe. Serve this egg salad in shot glasses or small cups as a snack or appetizer.

1. In a bowl, combine the eggs, onion, bell pepper, and jalapeño peppers.

2. Stir the Paleo Mayonnaise, white vinegar, lime juice, cumin, and sea salt into the egg mixture. Chill to combine the flavors before serving.

INGREDIENTS:

12 hard-boiled eggs, peeled and diced

½ cup diced white onion

½ red bell pepper, diced

10 pickled jalapeño pepper slices, diced

4 tablespoons Paleo Mayonnaise (page 267)

2 teaspoons white vinegar

1 teaspoon freshly squeezed lime juice

¼ teaspoon cumin

¼ teaspoon sea salt

DILL EGG

• • • SALAD • • •

 SERVES: 6   PREP TIME: 20 MIN.

This is a pretty standard version of egg salad. The dill and green onion add just enough of a twist to keep your palate entertained.

In a large bowl, combine the eggs, celery, green onions, Paleo Mayonnaise, mustard, dill, lemon juice, and sea salt. Chill to combine the flavors before serving.

INGREDIENTS:

12 hard-boiled eggs, peeled and chopped

½ cup chopped celery

3 green onions, sliced

3 tablespoons Paleo Mayonnaise (page 267)

2 teaspoons mustard

½ teaspoon dill

1 teaspoon freshly squeezed lemon juice

⅛ teaspoon sea salt

• • •

MIMOSA MUNCHIES

• • •

52

SAUSAGE MINI

• • • QUICHES • • •

INGREDIENTS:

½ pound Italian turkey sausage

2 cups chopped baby spinach

⅓ cup diced yellow onion

8 eggs

¼ teaspoon sea salt

½ teaspoon black pepper

Avocado oil in an oil mister

 SERVES: 6-8    PREP TIME: 15 MIN.    COOK TIME: 15 MIN.

Most Paleo followers are familiar with the frittata as a replacement for quiche. A frittata is basically a crustless quiche, and it's both protein-packed and delicious. By baking the frittata in a mini-muffin tin, you transform this Paleo staple into an elegant appetizer, and the flavorful sausage is a good trade-off for the lack of a crust!

1. Preheat the oven to 375°F.

2. In a large frying pan, cook the sausage over medium-high heat. As it cooks, continuously break apart the sausage until it crumbles. Remove the sausage from the pan, and set it aside in a large bowl.

3. In the same frying pan, add the spinach and onion. Sauté them over medium-high heat for 3-5 minutes or until soft. Drain any excess liquid, and add the spinach and onion to the bowl with the sausage.

4. Add the eggs, sea salt, and pepper to the sausage mixture, and stir until the ingredients are well blended.

5. Lightly spray a mini muffin tin with avocado oil. Fill the tin with the sausage and egg mixture until each cup is full to just below the rim. Bake the "quiches" for 15 minutes or until they are slightly browned and puffy on top.

6. Remove the "quiches" from the tin with a spoon before they are completely cool. Serve them warm or at room temperature.

• • •

MIMOSA MUNCHIES

54

RED, WHITE, AND BLUEBERRY

• • • SKEWERS • • •

 SERVES: 4-6   PREP TIME: 15 MIN.

INGREDIENTS:

4 large Fuji apples

2 tablespoons freshly squeezed
    lemon juice

9 ounces raspberries

9 ounces blueberries

Small wooden skewers

Tired of serving the standard fruit salad at breakfast? Dress it up with these patriotic fruit skewers! Berries are one of the healthiest fruit choices you can make, so feast guilt-free on this fruit dish.

1. Peel the apples. With a small melon baller, scoop out small balls from the apples.

2. Toss the apple balls in the lemon juice.

3. Thread each small skewer with a raspberry, an apple ball, and 2 blueberries. Serve chilled.

TIPS

If you don't have a melon baller, simply cube the apple instead.

Feel free to substitute your favorite fruits. Strawberries are a great alternative to raspberries. You can also use honeydew melon or banana in place of the apple.

MIMOSA MUNCHIES

56

APPETIZERS

TERIYAKI BEEF

• • • SKEWERS • • •

INGREDIENTS:

1½ pounds sirloin steak

1 tablespoon minced fresh ginger

2 cloves garlic, minced

1 teaspoon sesame seed oil

⅓ cup coconut aminos

⅓ cup water

1 pineapple

Wooden skewers

1 green onion, sliced

 SERVES: 4-6    PREP TIME: 15 MIN. (PLUS TIME TO MARINATE THE STEAK OVERNIGHT)    COOK TIME: 5-8 MIN.

These Teriyaki Beef Skewers bring all the flavors of the tropics to the party! The marinade is made with healthy, fresh ingredients and contains no added sugar or corn syrup. The grilled pineapple is the perfect sweet pairing for this sizzling dish.

1. Slice the steak lengthwise into ¼-inch strips, and set it aside.

2. In a large glass container, add the ginger, garlic, sesame seed oil, coconut aminos, and water to make the marinade. Stir to fully combine the ingredients. This is the marinade. Add the steak to the container, and refrigerate it in the marinade overnight.

3. Soak the skewers in water for 20 minutes.

4. Meanwhile, peel, core, and slice the pineapple into 1-inch slices.

5. Heat the grill to medium-high. Thread the steak strips onto the presoaked skewers, and grill the meat for 3 minutes. Turn the skewers, and grill the meat for an additional 3 minutes or until it reaches the desired doneness.

6. Remove the beef skewers, and grill the pineapple for 2 minutes per side, just enough to get some nice grill marks on it.

7. Garnish the beef with sliced green onion, and serve immediately with the grilled pineapple slices.

APPETIZERS

60

SCALLOP BACON
• • • SANDWICHES • • •

 SERVES: 4-5   PREP TIME: 15 MIN.   COOK TIME: 16 MIN.

These Scallop Bacon Sandwiches are definitely worthy of 5-Star Recipe status. Both the texture and the flavor of the scallops are greatly enhanced when they are quickly seared. After you sandwich some bacon, onion, and spinach between the split scallops, you are ready to add a dollop of sweet shallot sauce and prepare for a bite of pure heaven!

INGREDIENTS:

4 strips bacon

½ teaspoon curry powder

½ teaspoon cayenne pepper

¼ teaspoon sea salt

20 large scallops

Avocado oil in an oil mister

¼ cup thinly sliced red onion

½ cup baby spinach leaves, stems removed

SHALLOT SAUCE

1 tablespoon bacon grease

2 shallots, finely diced

4 tablespoons balsamic vinegar

¼ teaspoon honey

1. In a large frying pan over medium-high heat, cook the bacon until it is crisp, and then set it aside. Reserve 1 tablespoon of the bacon grease for the sauce.

2. In a small bowl, mix together the curry powder, cayenne pepper, and sea salt.

3. On a small plate, arrange the scallops in a single layer. Sprinkle half of the curry seasoning over the scallops. Place the scallops, seasoned side down, in a frying pan coated with cooking spray. Cook the scallops over medium-high heat for 3 minutes. Sprinkle the remaining seasoning onto the scallops, turn them, and cook them for another 3 minutes. Set the scallops aside.

4. In a medium-sized saucepan, make the sauce by combining the reserved bacon grease, shallots, balsamic vinegar, and honey. Simmer the mixture over medium-high heat until the sauce thickens.

5. Cut each scallop in half horizontally, and cut the bacon into 1-inch sections.

6. To assemble, start with half a scallop. Top it with a piece of bacon, a sliver of red onion, a leaf or two of spinach, and the other half of the scallop. Secure each stack with a toothpick, and finish with a small dollop of the shallot sauce.

APPETIZERS

62

INGREDIENTS:

4 tablespoons coconut aminos

4 tablespoons rice vinegar

1 tablespoon sesame seed oil

1-2 tablespoons chili paste

3 cloves garlic, minced

¼ teaspoon ground ginger

⅛ cup honey

½ teaspoon arrowroot powder

2 pounds chicken wings

Avocado oil in an oil mister

2 green onions, sliced

1 teaspoon sesame seeds

SPECIAL TOOLS:

 WIRE RACK

GENERAL TAO'S
• • • CHICKEN WINGS • • •

 SERVES: 4-6   PREP TIME: 10 MIN.   🔥 COOK TIME: 45 MIN.

If you enjoy General Tao's Chicken from Chinese restaurants, this is the appetizer for you. It takes the sweet, spicy sauce that you love and applies it to "finger-lickin' good" chicken wings. This dish is great either as an appetizer or as the basis of a light meal.

1. Preheat the oven to 400°F.

2. In a small saucepan, stir together the coconut aminos, rice vinegar, sesame seed oil, chili paste, garlic, ginger, and honey. Bring the mixture to a low boil over medium-high heat. Lightly sprinkle in the arrowroot powder while whisking continuously to avoid clumping. Simmer for 3 minutes until the sauce thickens. Add a little more arrowroot powder, if desired, to thicken the sauce further.

3. Rinse the chicken wings and pat them dry. Line a baking pan with foil. Place a wire rack on top of the pan, and spray it with avocado oil.

4. Brush the sauce onto the wings, and bake them for 20 minutes. Remove the wings from the oven, turn them over, and brush on more sauce. Bake them for another 20-25 minutes or until the skin is slightly crunchy. If necessary, broil them on high for 2 minutes to get the skin crispy.

5. Garnish the chicken wings with green onions and sesame seeds.

▶ TIPS ◀

This sauce is delicious, so if you're not a fan of wings, consider using it on chicken breasts or other meats, adjusting the baking time accordingly.

CHORIZO-STUFFED
• • • PEPPERS • • •

INGREDIENTS:

1 pound chorizo

½ white onion, diced

1 red bell pepper, diced

1 10-ounce can diced tomatoes
   with chilies, drained

3 tablespoons tomato paste

1 tablespoon chili powder

1 tablespoon cumin

1 teaspoon cayenne pepper

1 large bag miniature sweet
   peppers

GUACAMOLE

2 ripe avocados

1 teaspoon freshly squeezed
   lime juice

1 teaspoon garlic powder

1 jar sliced jalapeño peppers

 SERVES: 6-10   PREP TIME: 35 MIN.   COOK TIME: 20 MIN.

These poppable peppers have a subtle spice that is quickly cooled with a dollop of guacamole. However, if you're looking for extra zing, top them with pickled jalapeño peppers.

1. Preheat the oven to 375°F.

2. In a frying pan, cook the chorizo, crumbling it constantly with a spatula. Continue to stir and break up the chorizo until it is cooked through.

3. Add the onion, bell pepper, and tomatoes to the chorizo, and sauté them for 3 minutes. Drain the excess liquid, and add the tomato paste, chili powder, cumin, and cayenne pepper to the chorizo, stirring well to combine the ingredients.

4. Cut each miniature sweet pepper in half lengthwise. Discard any seeds, and fill each pepper with an ample serving of the chorizo mixture.

5. Place the stuffed peppers on a baking sheet, and bake for 15-20 minutes.

6. Meanwhile, in a bowl, mash together the avocado, lime juice, and garlic powder.

7. When the peppers are done, remove them from the oven, and let them cool for 5 minutes. Then top each pepper with a dollop of guacamole and a slice of jalapeño pepper.

TIPS

If you're short on time, serve the filling as a dip with the raw peppers.

Make this a dinner by filling poblano peppers with the chorizo stuffing and baking for 45 minutes.

• • •
APPETIZERS
• • •

INGREDIENTS:

15 large jalapeño peppers

2 ripe avocados

1 teaspoon garlic powder

½ teaspoon freshly squeezed lime juice

8 strips bacon

SPECIAL TOOLS:

 WIRE RACK

JALAPENO BACON
• • • POPPERS • • •

 SERVES: 3-5　　 PREP TIME: 15 MIN.　　 COOK TIME: 25 MIN.

Jalapeño Bacon Poppers are a fun way to spice up any party! While many guests will be familiar with this classic appetizer, this version is healthier than the cheese-filled, deep-fried variety. The creaminess of the avocado mimics the traditional cheese filling, and the bacon adds a crispy texture.

1. Preheat the oven to 425°F.

2. Wash the jalapeño peppers, cut them in half, and remove the seeds. Set them aside.

3. In a medium-sized bowl, mash the avocados well. Stir in the garlic powder and lime juice.

4. Spoon the avocado mixture into the jalapeño peppers.

5. Cut each strip of bacon in half lengthwise, and wrap the bacon around the jalapeños.

6. Line a baking pan with foil, and place a rack on top of the pan. Place the jalapeño poppers on top of the rack, and bake them for 20-25 minutes. To get the bacon extra crispy, broil the jalapeño poppers on high for 2 minutes. Let them cool for 2 minutes before serving.

FAJITA
• • • SKEWERS • • •

INGREDIENTS:

- 1 package chorizo chicken sausages
- 1 green bell pepper
- 1 yellow onion
- 1 tablespoon olive oil
- 1 teaspoon chili powder
- ½ teaspoon garlic powder
- ½ teaspoon cumin
- ½ teaspoon oregano
- ½ teaspoon crushed red pepper
- Large toothpicks
- ¼ cup finely chopped cilantro
- 1 avocado

 SERVES: 4   PREP TIME: 10 MIN.   COOK TIME: 15 MIN.

This easy, quick appetizer packs all the flavor of fajitas onto a skewer. While sausages can often be found on the appetizer table, the addition of tasty seasoned vegetables takes this dish to the next level.

1. Slice the chicken sausages into ¼-inch rounds. In a frying pan, cook them on medium-high heat until they are browned. Set them aside.

2. Cut the bell pepper in half, remove the seeds, and cut the bell pepper into 1-inch squares. Then peel the onion, and cut it into 1-inch squares.

3. In a separate frying pan, heat the olive oil on medium-high. Add the bell pepper, onion, chili powder, garlic powder, cumin, oregano, and crushed red pepper. Sauté the ingredients for 5-8 minutes until the vegetables are tender.

4. On large toothpicks, layer the ingredients. Start with a sausage round, then a piece of onion, and then a slice of bell pepper. Repeat this process on each toothpick, ending with a third piece of sausage. Sprinkle the skewers with cilantro, and serve with sliced avocado.

TIPS

Transform this dish into a dinner fajita salad by serving it over a bed of shredded lettuce and topping it with salsa as dressing.

SMOKY BACON-WRAPPED
• • • SHRIMP • • •

INGREDIENTS:

1 pound large shrimp, tails on

1 teaspoon chipotle chili powder

1 teaspoon onion powder

1 teaspoon garlic powder

1 teaspoon curry powder

½ teaspoon oregano

½ teaspoon paprika

¼ teaspoon cayenne pepper

1 pound bacon

Wooden skewers

 SERVES: 6-8   PREP TIME: 15 MIN.   COOK TIME: 25 MIN.

Combine two of my favorite edibles, bacon and shrimp, and the result is delectable. The seasoning adds a delicious smoky flavor. These crunchy bites of seafood are versatile enough for a formal occasion or a backyard barbecue.

1. Preheat the oven to 450°F.

2. Peel the shrimp, leaving the tails on. Place the shrimp in a single layer on a plate, and set them aside.

3. In a small bowl, combine the chipotle chili powder, onion powder, garlic powder, curry powder, oregano, paprika, and cayenne pepper. Sprinkle the mixture evenly over the shrimp.

4. Cut each strip of bacon in half lengthwise, and cut those strips in half again horizontally. Wrap each shrimp with bacon, and place approximately 3 bacon-wrapped shrimp on each skewer.

5. Line a baking pan with foil, and place a rack on top of it. Place the skewers on the rack, allowing space between pieces. Bake for 15-25 minutes or until the bacon is as crisp as you like. Halfway through, turn the skewers so that both sides of the bacon become crispy.

Alternative instructions: If you wish to grill the skewers rather than bake them, turn the grill to medium-high. Grill the skewers for 5 minutes per side. Keep an eye out for flare-ups, and make sure that the shrimp do not cook too quickly. Move the skewers to the top rack if necessary.

SPECIAL TOOLS:

 WIRE RACK

APPETIZERS

72

YELLOW CURRY

• • • SKEWERS • • •

 SERVES: 6-8   **PREP TIME: 15 MIN.**   **COOK TIME: 25 MIN.**

INGREDIENTS:

1 yellow onion

1 zucchini

2 red bell peppers

2 chicken breasts

15 mushrooms

1 pound large shrimp, tails on

½ lime

CURRY SAUCE

1 teaspoon fish sauce

1 tablespoon honey

1 13.5-ounce can full-fat coconut milk

2 cloves garlic, chopped

2 tablespoons chopped cilantro

1-3 tablespoons yellow curry paste

Small skewers

Yellow curry is an easy go-to for a yummy Paleo meal. Serving curry to guests can be tricky, however, because not everyone can handle the spice. Serving the sauce separately allows each guest to determine just how much they want to add to their personal skewer.

1. Preheat the oven to 400°F.

2. Cut the onion, zucchini, bell peppers, and chicken into 1-inch cubes. Cut the mushrooms in half.

3. Assemble the skewers by adding a slice of mushroom, zucchini, bell pepper, onion, and either a piece of chicken or shrimp to each.

4. Line a baking sheet with foil, and place the skewers on it. Squeeze the lime juice over the skewers, and bake them for 15 minutes. Then set the oven to broil, and broil the skewers for an additional 5-7 minutes until they are browned.

5. Meanwhile, prepare the sauce. In a small saucepan, stir together the fish sauce, honey, coconut milk, garlic, and cilantro. Stir in 1 tablespoon of the curry paste, then taste. Continue to add curry paste until you are happy with the amount of spice. Serve the sauce in a small bowl, allowing guests to add as much or as little as they please.

• • •
APPETIZERS
• • •

74

MINI DOGS

 SERVES: 8-10   PREP TIME: 25 MIN.   COOK TIME: 20 MIN.

Who doesn't love cocktail wieners? These are enhanced by a unique sauce that balances the slight sweetness of cranberries and orange juice with the heat of crushed red pepper. This easy dish can be prepared up to three days in advance and refrigerated until ready to cook. Read the label closely on the wieners, though, as some contain corn syrup. To ensure that you are purchasing quality meat, get some hot dogs from a local butcher, fully cook them, and serve them sliced with the sauce.

1. In a medium-sized saucepan over medium-high heat, cook the cranberries, red onion, tomato sauce, orange juice, honey, habañero pepper, garlic powder, crushed red pepper, white vinegar, and water. Stir the sauce until the berries are bursting and soft.

2. Transfer the sauce to a blender, and blend until smooth.

3. Add the cocktail wieners to the saucepan, along with enough sauce to generously coat them. Warm them over medium heat until they are heated through. Serve immediately on toothpicks or with utensils.

INGREDIENTS:

⅔ cup fresh cranberries

¼ cup finely chopped red onion

¼ cup tomato sauce

¼ cup fresh orange juice

2 tablespoons honey

1 habañero pepper, seeded and chopped

1 teaspoon garlic powder

¼ teaspoon crushed red pepper (or more for extra heat)

2 tablespoons white vinegar

¼ cup water

1 large package cocktail wieners

Toothpicks (optional)

SPECIAL TOOLS:

 BLENDER

· · · ·
APPETIZERS
· · · ·

76

PHILLY STEAK
• • • ROLL-UPS • • •

INGREDIENTS:

1 tablespoon olive oil

1½ yellow onions, thinly sliced

1 poblano pepper, seeded and thinly sliced

2 cloves garlic, chopped

2 large beef tenderloin steaks

½ teaspoon paprika

½ teaspoon chili powder

¼ teaspoon garlic powder

¼ teaspoon onion powder

¼ teaspoon thyme

Sea salt to taste

Black pepper to taste

Toothpicks

 SERVES: 4-6   PREP TIME: 15 MIN.   COOK TIME: 15 MIN.

These rolls capture the taste of Philly steak sandwiches without the bread and dairy. By using poblano peppers, you get an exciting kick that pairs nicely with the sweet caramelized onions.

1. In a large frying pan, heat the olive oil over medium heat. Add the onions, poblano pepper, and garlic to the warm olive oil. Sauté them until browned and caramelized, about 5-8 minutes. Remove the vegetables from the pan, and set them aside.

2. Slice the steak thinly, and place it in the frying pan. Sprinkle it with the paprika, chili powder, garlic powder, onion powder, thyme, sea salt, and pepper. Raise the heat to medium-high, and sauté the steak for 4 minutes.

3. To assemble the rolls, place a slice of poblano pepper and 2 slices of onion in the center of a slice of steak. Roll it closed, and secure it with a toothpick. Repeat the process with the remaining ingredients, and serve hot.

TIPS

If you desire an appetizer that's less spicy, substitute a green bell pepper for the poblano pepper.

SWEET POTATO SLICES

• • • WITH AVOCADO RANCH • • •

INGREDIENTS:

2 large sweet potatoes

3 tablespoons minced fresh rosemary

2 tablespoons minced garlic

1 tablespoon olive oil

¼ teaspoon sea salt

Avocado oil in an oil mister

5 strips bacon

3 green onions, sliced

AVOCADO RANCH

1 egg yolk

Extra-light olive oil

Reserved bacon grease

1 avocado

⅓ cup water

2 tablespoons fresh chives

1 teaspoon garlic powder

1 teaspoon dried parsley

1 teaspoon dried dill

½ teaspoon onion powder

1½ teaspoons apple cider vinegar

SPECIAL TOOLS:

 BLENDER

 SERVES: 4   PREP TIME: 15 MIN.   COOK TIME: 45 MIN.

After these sweet potato slices are seasoned and baked, they are topped with bacon, green onions, and a creamy Avocado Ranch dressing. Down a plate of these for dinner, or serve them at a football party. Your guests will end up cheering for more than their favorite team!

1. Preheat the oven to 400°F.

2. Scrub the sweet potatoes clean, and cut them into ¼-inch rounds. In a bowl, combine the sweet potatoes, rosemary, garlic, olive oil, and sea salt.

3. Line a baking sheet with foil, coat it with avocado oil, and spread the seasoned sweet potato rounds in a single layer on the foil. Bake the sweet potatoes for 20 minutes. Turn them over, and bake them for another 5-10 minutes.

4. Meanwhile, in a frying pan over medium-high heat, cook the bacon until it is crisp. Remove the bacon to dry on a paper towel, and reserve the grease. Chop the bacon, and set it aside.

5. To make the dip, place the egg yolk in a blender. Transfer the bacon grease to a glass measuring cup and add olive oil to ¼ cup line. With the blender on low, drizzle in the oil and bacon grease mixture. Do it very slowly to give it time to emulsify.

6. Turn off the blender, and add the avocado, water, chives, garlic powder, parsley, dill, onion powder, and apple cider vinegar. Blend until smooth.

7. Arrange the baked potatoes on a plate, and sprinkle them with the bacon and green onions. Then put half of the Avocado Ranch in a small plastic bag. Snip a small hole in a corner of the bag, and squirt the dip over the potatoes in a zigzag pattern. Serve the remaining dip on the side.

►◄ TIPS ►◄

To turn this dip into a salad dressing, add another ¼ cup water while blending.

• • • APPETIZERS • • •

80

BACON BRUSSELS SPROUT
• • • SKEWERS • • •

 SERVES: 6   PREP TIME: 15 MIN.   COOK TIME: 20 MIN.

When bacon and Brussels sprouts come together in this recipe, it's a clear case of opposites attracting. The healthy green sprouts take on all the salty flavor of the bacon, creating a taste sensation and an impressive presentation when assembled on a skewer.

INGREDIENTS:

1 pound bacon, thickly sliced

2 pounds Brussels sprouts

1 teaspoon ghee

1 teaspoon garlic powder

¼ teaspoon sea salt

Small wooden skewers

1. Cut each strip of bacon in half lengthwise. In a frying pan on medium heat, cook the bacon until it is partially cooked but still soft and pliable. (If you overcook the bacon, it will be difficult to weave it onto the skewer.) Remove the bacon from the pan, and set it aside. Remove most of the bacon grease from the pan, leaving just enough to coat it.

2. Cut the Brussels sprouts in half lengthwise. Add the Brussels sprouts, ghee, garlic powder, and sea salt to the frying pan. Sauté on medium-high heat until the sprouts are tender and browned.

3. Preheat the oven to 375°F.

4. Assemble the skewers by threading one end of the bacon onto the end of a skewer. Add a Brussels sprout slice, and weave the bacon around the sprout and back through the skewer. Move the bacon and the sprout down the skewer, and repeat this process 2 more times on each skewer. The bacon should create a wave pattern between the sprouts. Bake the skewers in a baking pan for 5-10 minutes or until the bacon is fully cooked.

INGREDIENTS:

1 pound bacon

½ cup shredded romaine lettuce

4 Roma tomatoes, finely diced

2 large cucumbers, thinly sliced

BACONNAISE

Reserved bacon grease

Extra-light olive oil

2 egg yolks

1 teaspoon apple cider vinegar

½ teaspoon mustard

½ teaspoon honey

¼ teaspoon sea salt

SPECIAL TOOLS:

 BLENDER

• • •
APPETIZERS
• • •

84

BLT CUCUMBER
• • • ROUNDS • • •

 SERVES: 8-10   PREP TIME: 10 MIN.   COOK TIME: 15 MIN.

Most Americans love a classic BLT sandwich. Substituting cucumber rounds for the bread creates a healthy Paleo version. The cucumbers also add a light, fresh taste that nicely offsets the rich bacon and mayonnaise topping.

1. In a frying pan over medium-high heat, cook the bacon until it is crisp. Remove the bacon from the pan, and reserve the grease in a 1-cup measuring cup. Add olive oil to fill to the 1 cup line.

2. In a blender, add the egg yolks, apple cider vinegar, mustard, honey, and sea salt. With the blender on its lowest setting, drizzle in the bacon grease-olive oil mixture. Pour it as slowly as possible to allow the mixture to emulsify.

3. Finely chop the cooked bacon. In a bowl, mix together the bacon, lettuce, and tomatoes with 2-3 tablespoons of the Baconnaise.

4. Arrange the cucumber slices on a platter, and top each round with a heaping spoonful of the bacon mixture.

TIPS

Prepare the bacon and Baconnaise up to 2 days ahead to shorten your prep time before serving.

BACON-WRAPPED
• • • WATER CHESTNUTS • • •

 SERVES: 4-8   **PREP TIME: 20 MIN.**   **COOK TIME: 45 MIN.**

INGREDIENTS:

2 8-ounce cans whole water chestnuts

Coconut aminos (or tamari)

1 pound bacon

¼ cup coconut sugar

Avocado oil in an oil mister

Toothpicks

Pretty much anything tastes delicious wrapped in bacon, but bacon-wrapped water chestnuts are my favorite. What a texture! While dates or scallops often end up mushy, water chestnuts have a welcome crunch. This recipe is both sweet and salty from the sugar and coconut aminos.

1. Preheat the oven to 400°F.

2. Drain the water chestnuts, and return them to their cans. Add coconut aminos to the cans until the water chestnuts are covered. Soak them for 15 minutes.

3. Cut the bacon strips in half lengthwise, and then in half again horizontally.

4. Place the coconut sugar in a small dish. Remove the water chestnuts, one at a time, from the cans, and roll them in the coconut sugar. Then wrap each water chestnut with a piece of bacon. Secure the bacon with a toothpick.

5. Spray a glass baking dish with avocado oil, and place the wrapped water chestnuts in the dish. Bake them for 30-35 minutes or until the bacon is crisp. When done, remove them from the dish, and let them cool for 5 minutes before serving.

TIPS

Drain some of the excess bacon grease while the water chestnuts are still cooking. Doing so will speed up the cooking time and ensure a crispier texture.

Because water chestnuts are not all uniform in size, you may wish to cut some of the larger ones in half. Doing so will also increase the number of pieces you serve – a good thing given how quickly this appetizer tends to disappear!

APPETIZERS

86

SPICY SAUSAGE-STUFFED
• • • MUSHROOMS • • •

INGREDIENTS:

1 pound hot Italian turkey or chicken sausage, casings removed

16 large mushrooms

4 cloves garlic, minced

⅔ cup diced yellow onion

1 cup chopped baby spinach

3 tablespoons Paleo Mayonnaise (page 267)

Avocado oil in an oil mister

 SERVES: 6-8   PREP TIME: 20 MIN.   COOK TIME: 24 MIN.

Spicy Italian sausage adds a little heat to these stuffed mushrooms, but the flavors are mild enough to please picky eaters. The creamy, smooth texture of the Paleo Mayonnaise can't be beat. It's a go-to appetizer for me!

1. Preheat the oven to 375°F.

2. In a large frying pan, cook the sausage, constantly breaking it apart with a spoon. Drain and discard any excess liquid, place the cooked sausage in a large bowl, and set it aside.

3. Wash the mushrooms, remove the stems. Reserve the caps, and finely chop the stems. Add the mushroom stems, garlic, onion, and spinach to the frying pan. Sauté the vegetables over medium-high heat until tender, about 4 minutes.

4. Add the vegetable mixture to the bowl of sausage, and stir in the Paleo Mayonnaise.

5. Spray a glass baking dish with avocado oil. Stuff the spinach-sausage mixture into each mushroom cap, and place them in the dish. Bake for 20 minutes.

6. Remove the mushrooms from the oven, and place them on a plate covered with a paper towel to absorb any excess liquid. Let them cool for a few minutes before serving.

TIPS

To make these mushrooms ahead of time, complete all of the steps except the final baking. Store them in the refrigerator for up to 2 days, and pop them in the oven on the day of the event.

TERIYAKI MEATBALL
• • • PINEAPPLE SKEWERS • • •

INGREDIENTS:
MEATBALLS

1 pound grass-fed ground beef

½ red onion, diced

⅓ cup diced red bell pepper

2 cloves garlic, minced

1 teaspoon ground ginger

Avocado oil in an oil mister

2 cups cubed fresh pineapple

Wooden skewers

TERIYAKI SAUCE

2 cups cubed fresh pineapple

½ cup coconut aminos (or tamari)

3 tablespoons honey

3 cloves garlic, minced

1 inch fresh ginger, peeled and minced

½ teaspoon sesame seed oil

½ teaspoon crushed red pepper

½ teaspoon arrowroot powder

SPECIAL TOOLS:

 BLENDER

 SERVES: 6-8   PREP TIME: 30 MIN.   COOK TIME: 35 MIN.

Add Asian flair to the classic cocktail meatball by coating the meat with this lush, thick teriyaki sauce. Top off each skewer with a bite of pineapple to satisfy your sweet tooth!

1. Preheat the oven to 400°F.

2. In a large bowl, mix together the ground beef, red onion, bell pepper, garlic, and ground ginger. Set it aside.

3. Line a baking pan with foil, and spray it with avocado oil. Form the beef mixture into 1½-inch balls, and place them on the baking sheet. Bake for 20 minutes.

4. Cut the pineapple into 1-inch cubes, reserving the juice. Set them aside.

5. To make the sauce, add the additional 2 cups of pineapple and any remaining juice, along with the coconut aminos, honey, garlic, ginger, sesame seed oil, and crushed red pepper, to a medium-sized saucepan. Sauté the mixture over high heat for 5 minutes.

6. Transfer the sauce to a blender, and purée it on high, with the blender vented, until smooth. Return the mixture to the saucepan, and heat it on medium-high heat.

7. When the sauce is hot, reduce the heat to low. Sprinkle the sauce with the arrowroot powder, and whisk as it simmers until the sauce thickens.

8. Preheat the broiler on high. Baste the meatballs with the teriyaki sauce. Broil the meatballs on the middle rack for 3-5 minutes or until they begin to brown on top.

9. Place a meatball on each skewer with a cube of pineapple on top. Serve with extra teriyaki sauce.

• • •
APPETIZERS

90

SMOKED SALMON BITES
• • • WITH LEMON-DILL AIOLI • • •

 SERVES: 4   PREP TIME: 15 MIN.   COOK TIME: 35 MIN.

These appetizers are as beautiful as they are tasty. Roll the salmon into little rosettes, and place it on sweet potato slices to impress your guests. The fresh, light Lemon-Dill Aioli perfectly complements the salmon.

INGREDIENTS:

SMOKED SALMON BITES

1 large, long, thin white sweet potato

1 tablespoon olive oil

1 teaspoon dried dill

½ teaspoon onion powder

½ teaspoon garlic powder

Avocado oil in an oil mister

1 8-ounce package sliced smoked salmon

LEMON-DILL AIOLI

1 egg

1 egg yolk

1 teaspoon mustard

3 teaspoons freshly squeezed lemon juice

½ cup bacon grease or coconut oil in a liquid state

⅔ cup extra-light olive oil

1½ tablespoons minced fresh dill

½ teaspoon garlic powder

SPECIAL TOOLS:

 BLENDER

1. Preheat the oven to 400°F.

2. Slice the sweet potato into ¼-inch rounds. Toss them with the olive oil, dried dill, onion powder, and garlic powder.

3. Line a baking sheet with foil, and coat it lightly with avocado oil. Spread out the sweet potato rounds on the sheet, making sure they don't overlap. Bake them for 20 minutes, turn them over, and bake them for an additional 5-10 minutes or until golden brown.

4. To prepare the aioli, add the egg, egg yolk, mustard, and lemon juice to a blender, and blend on low until combined.

5. Heat the bacon grease or coconut oil in the microwave for 10-15 seconds or until it is liquefied. With the blender on low, slowly drizzle the bacon grease or coconut oil into the blender. Next, drizzle the olive oil into the blender. Add the oils as slowly as possible to allow the mixture to emulsify.

6. Take ⅓ cup of the aioli, and add the dill and garlic powder to it. Store the remaining aioli for later use.

7. To assemble the bites, cut the smoked salmon into 1-inch pieces, and roll them into small rounds or rosettes. Place each salmon round on top of a potato slice, and garnish it with a dollop of the aioli.

• • • APPETIZERS

92

TIPS

The aioli can be made up to 2 days ahead. However, this dish is best served immediately out of the oven to prevent the potato rounds from becoming soggy.

SHRIMP
• • • COCKTAIL • • •

 SERVES: 8-10

PREP TIME: 5 MIN.
(PLUS 20 MINUTES TO CHILL)

Making your own cocktail sauce may seem labor-intensive, but it's worth it, especially since normal cocktail sauce contains high-fructose corn syrup. So whip up this zesty sauce whenever you want shrimp cocktail. It's ready in minutes and tastes like the real deal!

1. In a blender, blend the tomato paste, water, vinegar, lemon juice, horseradish, garlic, and honey on high until smooth.

2. Chill the sauce for 20 minutes before serving with the shrimp.

INGREDIENTS:

1 6-ounce can tomato paste

⅓ cup water

¼ cup white vinegar

⅛ cup freshly squeezed lemon juice

⅛ cup horseradish

1 clove garlic, minced

1 teaspoon honey

1 pound large shrimp, cooked, tails on

SPECIAL TOOLS:

 BLENDER

• • •
APPETIZERS
• • •

94

TIPS

Make the sauce up to 3 days ahead, but remember to stir it before serving.

BRUSCHETTA-STUFFED
• • • MUSHROOMS • • •

INGREDIENTS:

12 medium mushrooms

1 teaspoon ghee

1 Roma tomato, diced

1/3 cup diced white onion

4 cloves garlic, minced

1 tablespoon tomato paste

1/3 cup chopped fresh basil

1/8 teaspoon sea salt

1/8 teaspoon black pepper

3 slices prosciutto (optional)

 SERVES: 4   PREP TIME: 10 MIN.   🔥 COOK TIME: 20 MIN.

Bruschetta was one of my favorite non-Paleo appetizers. In this recipe, mushrooms replace the bread. Sprinkling chopped prosciutto on top adds a crispy finishing touch.

1. Preheat the oven to 375°F.

2. Remove the mushroom stems, and dice them. Set the caps aside.

3. In a medium-sized frying pan, melt the ghee over medium heat. Add the mushroom stems, tomato, onion, and garlic. Sauté the vegetables for 7 minutes or until they are cooked through and most of the liquid has evaporated.

4. In a small bowl, combine the cooked mushroom mixture with the tomato paste, basil, sea salt, and pepper. Spoon this mixture into each of the mushroom caps.

5. Cut the prosciutto (if using) into small slivers. Sprinkle the slivered prosciutto on top of the mushrooms. Place the mushrooms in a glass baking dish, and cook them for 25-30 minutes or until the mushrooms are tender and the prosciutto is browned.

CHORIZO SPANISH
• • • "TORTILLA" • • •

 SERVES: 10   PREP TIME: 20 MIN.   COOK TIME: 20 MIN.

INGREDIENTS:

1 large sweet potato

Avocado oil in an oil mister

½ pound chorizo

¾ yellow onion, sliced

2 jalapeño peppers, seeded and minced

2 cloves garlic, minced

7 eggs

1 avocado

This is not your typical Spanish tortilla! Chorizo adds protein as well as amazing flavor. You can serve this dish any way you please, in wedges or cubes. It's a great finger food because it's dense enough to pick up.

1. Preheat the oven to 400°F.

2. Peel the sweet potato and cut it into ¼-inch rounds.

3. Line a baking sheet with foil, and spray it with avocado oil. Spread the sweet potato rounds in a single layer on the sheet. Bake for 25-30 minutes or until the sweet potatoes are cooked through and browned.

4. In a large oven-safe frying pan, cook the chorizo, breaking it into small pieces with a spatula. Once the chorizo is cooked through, place it in a large bowl, and set it aside.

5. In the same frying pan, sauté the onion, jalapeño peppers, and garlic over medium-high heat until browned, about 8 minutes.

6. Add the sautéed vegetables to the bowl of chorizo, followed by the cooked sweet potatoes.

7. In a separate bowl, beat the eggs. Pour the eggs over the chorizo mixture, and fold them in. Return this mixture to the frying pan. Cover, and cook over medium heat for 5 minutes. Remove the lid, and place the pan in the oven for an additional 10-15 minutes or until the "tortilla" is firm on top.

8. Using a potholder to stabilize the pan, loosen the "tortilla" with a spatula and turn it onto a plate. Cut it into squares or small wedges, and garnish it with sliced or mashed avocado.

APPETIZERS

98

INGREDIENTS:

2 cucumbers

2 cups lump crab meat

5 tablespoons Paleo Mayonnaise (page 267)

1 avocado

Toothpicks

SPECIAL TOOLS:

 MANDOLINE

CRAB SALAD
• • • CUCUMBER ROLLS • • •

 SERVES: 4-6   PREP TIME: 10 MIN.

This light, refreshing recipe is simple to prepare. The Paleo Mayonnaise can be made ahead of time.

1. Thinly slice the cucumbers lengthwise using a mandoline, and set them aside.

2. Drain and squeeze out any excess liquid from the crab meat. In a bowl, stir together the crab and the Paleo Mayonnaise.

3. Slice the avocado.

4. To assemble the rolls, place a slice of avocado on one end of a slice of cucumber, followed by a small scoop of the crab mixture. Roll the cucumber around the mixture 1½ times. Trim off the excess cucumber, and secure the roll with a toothpick. Repeat with the remaining ingredients, and serve immediately.

◄ TIPS ►

If you are short on time or don't own a mandoline, make cucumber rounds instead of rolls. Just cut the cucumber into ¼-inch rounds, and top each with a spoonful of the crab salad and a slice of avocado.

MARINATED
• • • MUSHROOMS • • •

INGREDIENTS:

3 cups mushrooms

⅓ cup olive oil

⅓ cup red wine vinegar

4 cloves garlic, minced

2 tablespoons minced fresh thyme

1 tablespoon dried parsley

½ teaspoon ground mustard

¼ teaspoon sea salt

¼ teaspoon black pepper

 SERVES: 6-8   PREP TIME: 10 MIN.   🔥 COOK TIME: 10 MIN.

These mushrooms are marinated in a delicious blend of herbs and spices that excite the palate. Because they are so light, you can pair them with another richer appetizer or a heavy meal. They are also light on the budget compared to the cost of buying gourmet marinated mushrooms from the grocery store.

1. Wash and quarter the mushrooms.

2. In a medium-sized frying pan, combine the olive oil, red wine vinegar, garlic, thyme, parsley, mustard, sea salt, and pepper. Simmer over medium heat for 3 minutes. Add the mushrooms, and sauté them for an additional 10 minutes.

3. Transfer the mushrooms and the marinade to a container. Cover it, and chill it in the refrigerator until serving time.

APPETIZERS

TIPS

This recipe can be made 1-2 days before a party and served straight out of the fridge!

ANTIPASTO
• • • ROLL-UPS • • •

 SERVES: 10-12   PREP TIME: 15 MIN.

Antipasto platters are a staple at many events and are familiar to Paleo and non-Paleo guests alike. This recipe adds a tantalizing twist to the traditional platter. The presentation is beautiful, and the variety of flavor combinations is a unique experience for the taste buds.

1. Cut the turkey and ham slices in half, and set them aside.

2. Cut the asparagus and green beans in half, and set them aside.

3. Place 2 pepperoncini slices on one end of a slice of salami, and roll the salami closed. Place a black olive on a toothpick, and slide the toothpick through the salami roll. Repeat with the remaining salami, pepperoncini, and black olives.

4. Place 3 asparagus halves on one end of a slice of turkey, and roll the turkey closed. Place a kalamata olive on a toothpick, and slide the toothpick through the turkey roll. Repeat with the remaining turkey, asparagus, and kalamata olives.

5. Place 2 green beans pieces on one end of a slice of ham, and roll the ham closed. Place a garlic-stuffed olive on a toothpick, and slide the toothpick through the ham roll. Repeat with the remaining ham, green beans, and garlic-stuffed olives.

INGREDIENTS:

1 small package turkey slices, about 5-ounces

1 small package ham slices, about 5-ounces

1 jar pickled asparagus

1 jar spicy pickled green beans

1 jar sliced pepperoncini

1 small package salami slices

Toothpicks

1 can black olives

1 jar kalamata olives

1 jar garlic-stuffed green olives

TIPS

These roll-ups are easily made the day before and stored in the refrigerator until serving time.

APPETIZERS

104

PESTO-STUFFED
• • • TOMATOES • • •

INGREDIENTS:

1½ avocados

3 cloves garlic

6-8 basil leaves

½ teaspoon freshly squeezed lemon juice

¼ teaspoon sea salt

¼-½ cup water

20 cherry tomatoes

2 tablespoons pine nuts

 SERVES: 6-8   PREP TIME: 20 MIN.

Don't be fooled by the appearance of these bite-sized cherry tomatoes. They're anything but bland! They pack a flavor punch when stuffed with this spicy homemade pesto.

1. In a blender or food processor, blend the avocados, garlic, basil, lemon juice, sea salt, and ¼ cup water on high until smooth. If needed, add more water to achieve the desired consistency. Set the mixture aside.

2. Cut off the bottom of each tomato, and scoop out the insides. Place each tomato, cut side up, on a plate. Then use a spoon or pastry bag to fill each tomato with the avocado mixture.

3. Garnish the tomatoes with pine nuts, and serve them immediately.

SPECIAL TOOLS:

  BLENDER OR FOOD PROCESSOR

APPETIZERS

106

TIPS

The pesto-avocado cream will brown if not served right away.

SMALL PLATES

Petite PLATES WITH

Big Flavors!

SMALL PLATES

SPAGHETTI SQUASH

• • • FRITTERS WITH MEATBALLS • • •

INGREDIENTS:

FRITTERS

1 spaghetti squash

2 teaspoons minced garlic

1 teaspoon dried oregano

1 teaspoon dried basil

1 teaspoon onion powder

2 eggs

⅓ cup blanched almond flour

¼ teaspoon sea salt

¼ teaspoon black pepper

Avocado oil

MEATBALLS

Avocado oil in an oil mister

½ pound lean ground beef

½ pound ground Italian chicken sausage

SAUCE

1 6-ounce can tomato paste

1 cup water

½ cup canned crushed tomatoes

1 teaspoon garlic powder

1 teaspoon basil

1 teaspoon oregano

½ teaspoon thyme

½ teaspoon crushed red pepper

GARNISH

6 basil leaves, chopped

 SERVES: 4   PREP TIME: 45 MIN.   COOK TIME: 1 HR. 30 MIN.

While many people adore spaghetti squash, I personally don't care for its texture. However, when the spaghetti squash is fried, the resulting fritters have a fantastic crispy exterior that I enjoy. Topping these fritters with Italian-seasoned meatballs and marinara sauce produces a dish that I find positively irresistible!

1. Preheat the oven to 375°F. Pierce the squash several times with a sharp knife, and place it on a baking sheet. Bake for 50 minutes. When done, remove it, and set it aside to cool.

2. When the squash is cool, cut it in half. Scoop out and discard any pulp and seeds. With a fork, scrape out the squash meat into a large bowl. Stir in the garlic, oregano, basil, onion powder, eggs, almond flour, sea salt, and pepper.

3. Preheat a large frying pan over high heat, and coat it with avocado oil. Drop the squash mixture in 2-inch circles into the frying pan, and cook them on high for 3 minutes. Turn the fritters, and cook them for an additional 3 minutes on the other side.

4. Preheat the oven to 400°F. Line a baking sheet with foil, and spray it with avocado oil.

5. Mix together the ground beef and Italian sausage. Roll the meat mixture into 1½-inch balls, and place them on the baking sheet. Bake the meatballs for 20 minutes.

6. In a small saucepan, combine the tomato paste, water, crushed tomatoes, garlic powder, basil, oregano, thyme, and crushed red pepper. Add an additional ¼ teaspoon crushed red pepper for extra kick. Simmer on low.

7. To assemble, top each squash fritter with a spoonful of sauce and a meatball. Sprinkle each fritter with the chopped basil, and serve.

TIPS

Cook your spaghetti squash a day in advance. That way, it will already be cool and easy to handle.

EGGPLANT
• • • PIZZAS • • •

 SERVES: 4   PREP TIME: 40 MIN.   COOK TIME: 30 MIN.

INGREDIENTS:

CRUST

1 large eggplant

1 teaspoon sea salt

SAUCE

1 6-ounce can tomato paste

1¼ cups water

1 teaspoon garlic powder

1 teaspoon dried basil

½ teaspoon dried oregano

½ teaspoon dried thyme

½ teaspoon dried rosemary

¼ teaspoon sea salt

TOPPINGS

½ pound Italian sausage

Avocado oil in an oil mister

1 5-ounce package pepperoni

½ green bell pepper, diced

¼ red onion, diced

1 6-ounce can sliced black olives, drained

4 basil leaves, chopped

Crushed red pepper to taste

Who doesn't love pizza? Of course, within the confines of a Paleo lifestyle, it's hard to imagine how you could capture the essence of a pizza. An almond flour crust is still calorie-dense, full of fat, and could not be served to those with nut allergies. So why not try using eggplant? These individual-sized eggplant pizzas are the perfect alternative!

1. Slice the eggplant into ½-inch rounds. Place the eggplant on a paper towel, and sprinkle it with the sea salt. Let it stand for 30 minutes, and pat it dry.

2. In a small bowl, prepare the sauce. Combine the tomato paste, water, garlic powder, basil, oregano, thyme, rosemary, and sea salt.

3. In a frying pan, brown and crumble the Italian sausage over medium-high heat.

4. Preheat the oven to 375°F. Spray a baking sheet with avocado oil, and place the eggplant rounds on the sheet. Top each round with sauce, cooked sausage, pepperoni, bell pepper, onions, and olives. Bake for 25 minutes or until the eggplant is tender but not soggy.

5. Remove the pizzas from the oven, and top them with the chopped basil and crushed red pepper.

TIPS

Instead of using eggplant, you could use zucchini strips or portobello mushrooms as a base.

SMALL PLATES

112

CRAB CAKES WITH
• • • WASABI-AVOCADO SAUCE • • •

INGREDIENTS:

CRAB CAKES

1 pound lump crab meat, drained

¼ cup minced red bell pepper

3 green onions, thinly sliced

2 egg yolks

⅛ cup Paleo Mayonnaise (page 267) (optional)

½ teaspoon garlic powder

¼ teaspoon onion powder

Dash cayenne pepper

½ teaspoon sea salt

¼ teaspoon black pepper

⅛ cup blanched almond flour

⅛ cup unsweetened shredded coconut

2 tablespoons coconut oil

WASABI-AVOCADO SAUCE

1 avocado

1-2 teaspoons wasabi paste (or more to taste)

⅓ cup water

1 tablespoon coconut aminos

1 tablespoon rice vinegar

⅛ teaspoon sea salt

SPECIAL TOOLS:

 BLENDER

 SERVES: 2-4 PREP TIME: 20 MIN. COOK TIME: 10 MIN.

These coconut-crusted crab cakes will exceed your expectations! They are seasoned to perfection, crispy, and brimming with succulent crab. The Wasabi-Avocado Sauce offers a creamy, zesty topping for this already superior dish.

1. In a medium-sized bowl, mix together the crab meat, bell pepper, green onions, egg yolks, Paleo Mayonnaise (if using), garlic powder, onion powder, cayenne pepper, sea salt, and black pepper. Form the mixture into 3-inch patties, and place them on a plate. Refrigerate them for 15 minutes.

2. In a small dish, mix together the almond flour and shredded coconut, and set the mixture aside.

3. In a large skillet, heat the coconut oil on high. Remove the crab patties from the refrigerator, and coat both sides with the almond flour and coconut mixture, brushing off any excess. Cook the patties for 4 minutes per side or until golden brown and crispy.

4. To make the sauce, combine the avocado, wasabi paste, water, coconut aminos, rice vinegar, and sea salt in a blender. Blend on high until smooth.

5. Serve the crab cakes hot with a drizzle or dollop of the Wasabi-Avocado Sauce.

TACO SLIDERS WITH
• • • CHIPOTLE AIOLI • • •

 SERVES: 3-4   PREP TIME: 15 MIN.   COOK TIME: 8 MIN.

These little burgers will have you dancing the salsa. The grass-fed beef is seasoned like taco meat and topped with a kickin' Chipotle Aioli. Serve these burgers with some plantain chips and guacamole on the side for a fantastic fiesta!

INGREDIENTS:

TACO SLIDERS

1½ pounds grass-fed ground beef

1 tablespoon chili powder

1 teaspoon cumin

½ teaspoon garlic powder

¼ teaspoon onion powder

½ teaspoon cayenne pepper

¼ teaspoon paprika

CHIPOTLE AIOLI

1 egg yolk

1 teaspoon apple cider vinegar

1 teaspoon mustard

⅔ cup extra-light olive oil

1 clove garlic, chopped

⅛ teaspoon sea salt

1 teaspoon honey

2-3 chipotle chilies in adobo sauce

½ jalapeño pepper, seeded and diced

TOPPINGS

1 head butter lettuce

½ avocado, sliced

¼ red onion, diced

SPECIAL TOOLS:

 BLENDER

1. In a bowl, mix together the ground beef, chili powder, cumin, garlic powder, onion powder, cayenne pepper, and paprika. Form the mixture into 10 small patties, pressing a small thumbprint in the center of each one. Grill or pan-fry the patties for 3 minutes per side.

2. To make the Chipotle Aioli, combine the egg yolk, apple cider vinegar, and mustard in a blender, and blend on low. Drizzle in the olive oil as slowly as possible to allow it to emulsify. Add the garlic, sea salt, honey, chipotle chilies, and jalapeño pepper, and blend the mixture on high until it is smooth.

3. Place each burger on top of a piece of butter lettuce. Top with 1 tablespoon of the Chipotle Aioli, a slice of avocado, and pieces of red onion.

INGREDIENTS:

MINI MEATLOAVES

1 pound grass-fed lean ground beef

7 strips bacon, cooked and chopped

½ yellow onion, diced

¼ red bell pepper, diced

1 egg

¼ cup pork rinds, ground

1 tablespoon chili powder

BARBECUE SAUCE

½ teaspoon olive oil

½ yellow onion, diced

6 cloves garlic, minced

1 6-ounce can tomato paste

2 cups beef broth

4 dates, pitted and diced

2 tablespoons spicy brown mustard

2 tablespoons apple cider vinegar

1 tablespoon chili powder

1 teaspoon cumin

½ teaspoon liquid smoke

½ teaspoon sea salt

MASHED "POTATO" TOPPING

½ head cauliflower, chopped

½ white sweet potato, chopped

2 cloves garlic

½ teaspoon sea salt

½ teaspoon black pepper

BARBECUE BACON
• • • MINI MEATLOAVES • • •

 SERVES: 4   PREP TIME: 45 MIN.   COOK TIME: 35 MIN.

Say hello to a trifecta of flavors with this barbecue sauce, bacon, and cauliflower-topped meatloaf. It doesn't get more loaded than this! Your guests will feel extra special when they are served a mini meatloaf of their own.

1. Preheat the oven to 375°F.

2. In a large bowl, mix together the ground beef, bacon, onion, bell pepper, egg, pork rinds, and chili powder. Divide the mixture into 4 mini roasting pans or 6-8 muffin cups if using a muffin tin. Bake for 25 minutes.

3. Meanwhile, prepare the barbecue sauce. In a small saucepan, heat the olive oil. Add the onion and garlic to the pan, and sauté them for 2 minutes. Stir in the tomato paste, beef broth, dates, mustard, apple cider vinegar, chili powder, cumin, liquid smoke, and sea salt. Simmer for 5 minutes.

4. In a blender, add the sauce, blend it on high until smooth. Transfer the sauce to a bowl, and set it aside.

5. Steam the cauliflower, sweet potato, and garlic for 12 minutes. Drain, and let cool.

6. In a food processor, purée the cauliflower, sweet potato, garlic, sea salt, and pepper. Remove the mixture, and place it in a pastry bag or bowl.

7. Top each meatloaf with a tablespoon of barbecue sauce and some of the cauliflower mashed "potato" topping. Broil the meatloaves on high for 3-5 minutes or until slightly browned. Serve with extra barbecue sauce, if desired.

SPECIAL TOOLS:

 BLENDER   FOOD PROCESSOR

INGREDIENTS:

RIBS

⅓ cup pickling spice

1 teaspoon parsley flakes

1 teaspoon onion flakes

1 teaspoon sage, dried

2 bay leaves, crumbled

Cheesecloth

Cotton string or thread

2 racks baby back pork ribs (about 2.5 pounds)

Avocado oil in an oil mister

BARBECUE SAUCE

½ teaspoon olive oil

½ yellow onion, chopped

6 cloves garlic, minced

1 6-ounce can tomato paste

2 cups beef broth

4 dates, pitted and diced

2 tablespoons spicy brown mustard

2 tablespoons apple cider vinegar

1 tablespoon chili powder

1 teaspoon cumin

½ teaspoon liquid smoke

1 teaspoon sea salt

SPECIAL TOOLS:

 BLENDER

AUNT ESTHER'S
• • • FAMOUS RIBS • • •

 SERVES: 4-6   PREP TIME: 15 MIN.
(PLUS 2 HOURS TO MARINATE THE RIBS)   🔥 COOK TIME: 1 HOUR 20 MINS.

This is a tried-and-true, "fall-off-the-bone" rib recipe. Boiling the ribs with the spice bouquet first gives the meat a rich base of flavor even before the barbecue sauce is applied. This Paleo version is based on my Aunt Esther's ribs, a longstanding family favorite.

1. Make a spice bouquet by placing the pickling spice, parsley flakes, onion flakes, sage, and bay leaves in the center of a piece of cheesecloth. Tie the cheesecloth closed with the string.

2. Fill a large pot with water, and bring the water to a boil.

3. Cut the ribs apart, and trim any excess fat. Add the ribs and the spice bouquet to the boiling water. Return the water to a boil, reduce the heat, and simmer for 35 minutes.

4. To make the sauce, heat the olive oil in a small saucepan over medium-high heat. Sauté the onion and garlic for 2 minutes. Mix in the tomato paste, beef broth, dates, mustard, apple cider vinegar, chili powder, cumin, liquid smoke, and sea salt. Simmer for 5 minutes.

5. Move sauce mixture to a blender and blend on high until smooth. Transfer the sauce to a bowl, and set it aside.

6. Line a baking sheet with foil, and spray it with avocado oil. Drain the ribs, and brush them with the barbecue sauce. Place them on the baking sheet, and refrigerate them for 2 hours.

7. Preheat the oven to 350°F.

8. Once the ribs are cool, brush them again with the sauce. Bake them for 40-45 minutes or until browned.

SMALL PLATES

120

LEMON CHICKEN SKEWERS
• • • WITH ALMOND SATAY SAUCE • • •

INGREDIENTS:

LEMON CHICKEN

1 tablespoon olive oil

4 large chicken breasts

¼ teaspoon sea salt

¼ teaspoon black pepper

3 tablespoons freshly squeezed lemon juice

Wooden skewers

ALMOND SATAY SAUCE

1 tablespoon sesame oil

⅔ cup diced red onion

2 large cloves garlic, minced

1 tablespoon peeled and minced fresh ginger

½ cup almond butter

⅓ cup tomato sauce

2 tablespoons coconut aminos

2 tablespoons red wine vinegar

½ teaspoon crushed red pepper

1 tablespoon honey

Juice of ½ lime

¼-¾ cup water

   SERVES: 4-6   PREP TIME: 20 MIN.   COOK TIME: 35 MIN.

Enjoy the Thai flavors as sweet satay sauce tames tart lemon chicken. These skewers can be served as an appetizer or an entrée, so don't hesitate to make them for any occasion.

1. Preheat the oven to 325°F.

2. In a large oven-safe frying pan, heat the olive oil on medium-high. Sprinkle the chicken with sea salt and pepper, and add the chicken to the pan. Pour the lemon juice over the chicken, and cook it for 3 minutes. Turn the chicken, and cook it for an additional 3 minutes.

3. Place the pan in the oven, and bake the chicken for 15 minutes or until it is no longer pink in the middle. When done, remove the chicken from the oven, and let it cool. Cut the chicken into ½-inch slices, and thread the slices onto the skewers. Set the skewers aside.

4. In a medium-sized saucepan, start the sauce by heating the sesame oil. Add the onion, garlic, and ginger to the pan, and sauté them over medium-high heat for 3-5 minutes or until the onion is translucent. Stir in the almond butter, tomato sauce, coconut aminos, red wine vinegar, crushed red pepper, honey, and lime juice. Reduce the heat to low, and stir. Slowly add the water ¼ cup at a time, stirring constantly, until the sauce reaches the desired consistency.

5. Serve the chicken warm or at room temperature with a bowl of the warm satay sauce.

TIPS

If you prefer a smooth satay sauce, put the sauce into a blender and purée it before serving.

SMALL PLATES

122

ASIAN CHICKEN LETTUCE CUPS
• • • WITH GRAPE "HOISIN" SAUCE • • •

INGREDIENTS:

1 head iceberg lettuce

2 green onions, sliced

CHICKEN

1 teaspoon olive oil

2 large chicken breasts

1 teaspoon sesame seed oil

5 mushrooms, diced

2 cloves garlic, minced

1 teaspoon minced fresh ginger

1 8-ounce can sliced water chestnuts, drained and diced

1 8-ounce can bamboo shoots, drained and diced

3 tablespoons coconut aminos

1 tablespoon rice vinegar

1 teaspoon Sriracha sauce (optional)

1 teaspoon honey

GRAPE "HOISIN" SAUCE

2 cups halved grapes

2 cloves garlic, minced

2 shallots, minced

1 teaspoon minced fresh ginger

2 tablespoons coconut aminos

½ teaspoon Chinese Five-Spice

SPECIAL TOOLS:

 BLENDER

 SERVES: 4    PREP TIME: 15 MIN.   COOK TIME: 20 MIN.

If you've ever enjoyed the chicken lettuce wraps at P.F. Chang's, you will love these lettuce cups! All the traditional Asian flavors are present, including a sweet grape sauce that mimics hoisin.

1. In a large frying pan, heat the olive oil. Fillet the chicken, and cook it over medium-high heat for 4-5 minutes per side or until it is no longer pink in the middle. Remove the chicken from the pan, and cut it into ½-inch cubes. Set it aside.

2. Heat the sesame seed oil in the frying pan, and add the mushrooms, garlic, and ginger. Sauté for 3 minutes. Add the water chestnuts, bamboo shoots, coconut aminos, rice vinegar, Sriracha sauce (if using), and honey. Sauté the mixture for another 5 minutes. Return the chicken to the pan with the sauce, and reduce the heat to low.

3. To make the sauce, place the grapes, garlic, shallots, and ginger in a medium-sized saucepan. Cook on high heat for 5 minutes. Add the coconut aminos and Chinese Five-Spice, bring the mixture to a boil, and cook it for 3 more minutes.

4. Transfer the mixture to a blender, and blend until the sauce is smooth.

5. Separate the lettuce leaves. Fill each leaf with the chicken mixture, top it with a tablespoon of the grape sauce, and sprinkle it with green onions. Serve with any remaining sauce.

SMALL PLATES

124

LAMB DOLMAS WITH
• • • EGG-LEMON SAUCE • • •

 SERVES: 4-6   PREP TIME: 40 MIN.   🔥 COOK TIME: 1 HR.

My Aunt Elaine is Greek and a great cook, so I had the pleasure of being exposed to Greek food while I was growing up. Dolmas are among my favorite dishes. These grape leaves are filled with seasoned lamb and buttery pine nuts and topped with a decadent lemon sauce. Although this recipe is labor-intensive, the results are worth it!

1. In a large skillet, heat the olive oil on medium heat. Add the yellow onions to the pan, and sauté them for 3 minutes. Increase the heat to medium-high, and add the ground lamb. Sauté and break up the lamb with a spoon until it is no longer pink.

2. In a food processor, pulse the cauliflower until it is the consistency of rice. Add the cauliflower "rice" to the skillet, and sauté it for 3 minutes. Skim off any excess liquid.

3. In a large bowl, combine the pine nuts, green onions, parsley, mint, allspice, cinnamon, sea salt, and pepper. Add the lamb mixture to the bowl, and stir.

4. Drain and rinse the grape leaves, and place them on a paper towel. Trim off any remaining stems. Spoon 1-2 tablespoons of the lamb mixture on one side of each leaf. Roll tightly, folding in the edges of the leaf like a burrito.

5. Spray a large frying pan with avocado oil. Place the stuffed grape leaves, seam side down, in the pan. Turn the heat to high. Pour the chicken broth over the dolmas, bring to a boil, reduce the heat to low, cover, and simmer for 1 hour.

6. While the dolmas cook, make the Egg-Lemon Sauce. Separate the egg yolks from the egg whites into 2 medium-sized bowls. Add the lemon juice to the egg yolks, and whisk.

7. In a separate bowl, whisk the egg whites until they are frothy.

8. Heat the chicken broth in the microwave for 30 seconds. Then whisk the warm broth into the egg yolk mixture.

9. Stir in the egg whites. Add the mixture to a small saucepan on medium-high heat. Stir until the sauce thickens, and reduce the heat to low. Stir in the honey (if using). If the sauce isn't thick enough, sprinkle in ½ teaspoon arrowroot powder, and whisk.

10. Arrange the dolmas on a platter, and pour the sauce on top. Serve warm.

INGREDIENTS:

LAMB DOLMAS

1 tablespoon olive oil

1 cup diced yellow onion

1 pound ground lamb

1 cup cauliflower florets

¼ cup pine nuts

3 green onions, sliced

1 tablespoon minced fresh parsley

2 teaspoons minced fresh mint

½ teaspoon allspice

½ teaspoon cinnamon

½ teaspoon sea salt

½ teaspoon black pepper

1 16-ounce jar grape leaves in brine

Avocado oil in an oil mister

1 cup chicken broth

EGG-LEMON SAUCE

2 eggs

Juice of 1½ lemons

1 cup chicken broth

1 tablespoon honey (optional)

½ teaspoon arrowroot powder (if needed)

SPECIAL TOOLS:

 FOOD PROCESSOR

• • •
SMALL PLATES

126

EGGPLANT SAUSAGE

• • • SLIDERS • • •

 SERVES: 4   ⏰ PREP TIME: 20 MIN.   🔥 COOK TIME: 30 MIN.

Crispy eggplant rounds make a terrific base for Italian sausage. Top them with fresh basil and marinara sauce for a tasty dinner or starter course.

INGREDIENTS:

SLIDERS

1 large eggplant

Sea salt to taste

1 egg

2 tablespoons water

½ cup blanched almond flour

1½ teaspoons dried basil

¼ teaspoon fresh garlic

¼ teaspoon dried thyme

½ teaspoon dried oregano

Avocado oil in an oil mister

1 pound Italian chicken
   sausage

1 bunch fresh basil, chopped

SIMPLE TOMATO SAUCE

1 cup tomato sauce

1 teaspoon garlic powder

1 teaspoon dried basil

½ teaspoon dried rosemary

1 teaspoon dried oregano

½ teaspoon sea salt

1. Preheat the oven to 375°F.

2. Slice the eggplant into ¼-inch rounds, and lay the slices on a paper towel. Sprinkle them with salt, and let them stand for 20 minutes.

3. In a shallow dish, scramble the egg with the water, and set the mixture aside.

4. In another shallow dish, mix together the almond flour, basil, garlic, thyme, and oregano. Set the mixture aside.

5. Line a baking sheet with foil, and spray it with avocado oil. Dip both sides of the eggplant in the egg mixture. Then lightly press both sides of the eggplant into the almond flour mixture. Shake off the excess flour, and place the eggplant rounds on the baking sheet.

6. Bake the eggplant rounds for 15 minutes, turn them over, and bake them for another 10 minutes. Place the eggplant on the top rack and broil them for 2-3 minutes until slightly browned.

7. Meanwhile, divide the sausage into 8 small patties, and cook them in a large frying pan over medium-high heat for 3-5 minutes per side or until cooked through.

8. In a microwave-safe bowl, stir together the tomato sauce, garlic powder, basil, rosemary, oregano, and sea salt. Cover the bowl with plastic wrap, and microwave it for 30 seconds. Stir, and microwave it for another 30 seconds.

9. To assemble the sliders, top each eggplant round with a sausage patty and some marinara sauce. Sprinkle each slider with the chopped basil, and serve them immediately.

SMALL PLATES

128

LAMB LOLLIPOPS WITH
• • • APRICOT-BALSAMIC GLAZE • • •

 SERVES: 4-6   PREP TIME: 15 MIN.   COOK TIME: 15 MIN.

INGREDIENTS:

LAMB LOLLIPOPS

24 baby lamb chops

2 tablespoons olive oil

4 cloves garlic, minced

3 tablespoons chopped fresh rosemary

1 tablespoon fresh thyme

APRICOT-BALSAMIC GLAZE

½ cup puréed apricots

2 tablespoons honey

¼ cup balsamic vinegar

⅛ cup water

1 teaspoon minced fresh thyme

½ teaspoon crushed red pepper

These bite-sized lamb lollipops are an extremely fancy dish that you would serve at a five-star event. Drizzled with Apricot-Balsamic Glaze, these tender chops will surely wow your guests!

1. Trim any excess fat from the lamb chops, and set them aside.

2. In a bowl, stir together the olive oil, garlic, rosemary, and thyme. Rub the mixture on the lamb chops, and refrigerate them for 20 minutes.

3. In a small saucepan, stir together the apricots, honey, balsamic vinegar, and water. Bring the mixture to a boil, and cook for 5 minutes. Add the thyme and crushed red pepper, and reduce the heat. Simmer for 10 minutes.

4. Broil the lamb chops on high for 4 minutes per side on the top rack, about 4 inches from the broiler. If the lamb chops are thick they may require longer. Serve the chops drizzled with the Apricot-Balsamic Glaze.

PALEO

• • • SUSHI • • •

 SERVES: 4   PREP TIME: 20 MIN.

INGREDIENTS:

1 cup lump crab meat

3 tablespoons Paleo Mayonnaise (page 267), divided

24 medium shrimp, cooked

1 carrot

1 cucumber

4 green onions

4 sheets nori (seaweed paper)

1 avocado

1½ tablespoons Sriracha sauce

Wasabi paste

Coconut aminos

While cavemen may not have eaten sushi, traditional sushi ingredients are primarily Paleo, except for the rice. I created this sushi recipe without rice so that you can indulge in this popular Asian delicacy without guilt.

1. Drain the crab meat, and squeeze out any remaining liquid. In a bowl, combine 1 tablespoon of the Paleo Mayonnaise and the crab meat.

2. Straighten out the shrimp by cutting shallow horizontal slices into the arch of each shrimp and pressing it flat. Set the shrimp aside.

3. Julienne the carrot and cucumber, and slice the green onion into long, thin strips.

4. To assemble the sushi, put a piece of nori on top of a piece of plastic wrap. Place the carrot, cucumber, and green onion along the length of the edge closest to you. Layer 8 shrimp on top of the carrot, cucumber, and green onion. Spoon ¼ cup of the crab mixture beside the row you just created. Slice a quarter of the avocado on top of the crab mixture, and tightly roll the seaweed around the contents. Using your finger, dab water along the outer edge of the nori to seal it closed. Using a very sharp knife, slice the roll into 1-inch rounds. Repeat this process with the remaining ingredients.

5. In a small bowl, stir together the remaining 2 tablespoons mayonnaise and the Sriracha sauce. Drizzle the mixture over the sushi, and serve it with wasabi paste and coconut aminos.

SMALL PLATES

132

CRAB-STUFFED MINI
• • • PORTOBELLO MUSHROOMS • • •

SMALL PLATES

INGREDIENTS:

12 mini portobello mushrooms (or 16 large white mushrooms)

1 tablespoon ghee

½ red bell pepper, diced

2 green onions, sliced

¼ teaspoon garlic powder

¼ teaspoon paprika

¼ teaspoon onion powder

⅛ teaspoon dried thyme

⅛ teaspoon dried oregano

Dash cayenne pepper

2 cups lump crab meat

3 tablespoons Paleo Mayonnaise (page 267)

Avocado oil in an oil mister

 SERVES: 4-6   PREP TIME: 10 MIN.   COOK TIME: 20 MIN.

This decadent dish combines two of my favorite delicacies—crab and portobello mushrooms. Packed with protein, these appetizers will surely be a hit with the seafood lovers on your guest list.

1. Preheat the oven to 400°F.

2. Wash the mushrooms, and remove the stems. Set the caps aside. Finely dice the stems, and set them aside.

3. In a frying pan, melt the ghee over medium-high heat. Add the mushroom stems, bell pepper, and green onions, and sauté for 3 minutes until the vegetables are tender. Add the garlic powder, paprika, onion powder, thyme, oregano, and cayenne pepper, and sauté for 1 minute.

4. In a medium-sized bowl, stir together the crab meat and Paleo Mayonnaise. Then add the mushroom mixture, and stir.

5. Spray a 9 x 13-inch glass casserole dish with avocado oil. Stuff each mushroom cap with the crab mixture, and place them in the dish. Bake for 15-20 minutes until the mushroom caps are tender.

6. Cover a serving plate with a paper towel, and place the mushrooms on top to absorb any excess liquid before serving.

INGREDIENTS:

CURRY CHICKEN PATTIES

1 pound ground chicken

½ red onion, diced

¼ red bell pepper, diced

1½ tablespoons green curry paste

Avocado oil in an oil mister

1 cup coleslaw

CILANTRO-LIME AIOLI

⅓ cup Paleo Mayonnaise (page 267)

1 teaspoon green curry paste

2 teaspoons freshly squeezed lime juice

2 tablespoons chopped cilantro

CURRY CHICKEN PATTIES
• • • WITH CILANTRO-LIME AIOLI • • •

 SERVES: 3-4   PREP TIME: 15 MIN.   COOK TIME: 20 MIN.

Green curry paste adds a jolt to these chicken patties. Served with Cilantro-Lime Aioli, this spicy dish is perfect if you are craving curry but prefer something lighter without coconut milk.

1. In a large bowl, stir together the ground chicken, red onion, bell pepper, and curry paste. Form the mixture into 2-inch patties.

2. Heat a large skillet over medium-high heat, and spray it with avocado oil. Cook the chicken patties for 3-4 minutes per side or until cooked through.

3. In a small bowl, make the Cilantro-Lime Aioli by stirring together the Paleo Mayonnaise, curry paste, lime juice, and cilantro. Set it aside.

4. Spread the coleslaw on a serving platter, and top it with the hot chicken patties. Spoon the aioli over the chicken patties, or serve it on the side.

SMALL PLATES

136

TUNA TARTARE
• • • TOWERS • • •

INGREDIENTS:

TOWERS

1 pound sushi-grade ahi tuna

1 teaspoon olive oil

½ teaspoon sesame seed oil

4 tablespoons coconut aminos

1-3 teaspoons wasabi paste (depending on desired spiciness)

1 teaspoon Sriracha sauce

1 teaspoon freshly squeezed lime juice, divided

2 green onions, sliced

4 avocados, diced

SAUCE

4 tablespoons coconut aminos

1 teaspoon wasabi paste

1 teaspoon Sriracha sauce

 SERVES: 4   PREP TIME: 15 MIN.

There is nothing better than fresh raw tuna, except possibly tuna tartare. When you layer it with avocado and pair it with a spicy sauce, you create a tower of power. Eat this dish with a fork, or serve it as a dip with your favorite Paleo chip recipe.

1. Cube the tuna into ½-inch cubes. Place the tuna in a bowl, and add the olive oil, sesame seed oil, coconut aminos, wasabi paste, Sriracha sauce, ½ teaspoon of the lime juice, and green onions. Stir the mixture until it is completely combined.

2. In a separate bowl, mix the avocados with the remaining ½ teaspoon lime juice, and set them aside.

3. In a separate small bowl, make the sauce by whisking together the coconut aminos, wasabi paste, and Sriracha sauce.

4. To plate the towers, press some of the avocado mixture into a round cookie cutter. Make a round of the tuna mixture, and press it on top of the avocado. Arrange the completed towers on a platter, and drizzle the sauce around them.

INGREDIENTS:

MANGO GAZPACHO

2 ripe mangoes, peeled and pitted

2 cups fresh orange juice

3 tablespoons freshly squeezed lime juice

2 cloves garlic

1½ jalapeño peppers, seeded and chopped

½ red bell pepper, chopped

¾ cucumber, seeded and chopped

¼ cup sliced green onions

⅛ cup cilantro

BLACKENED SHRIMP

1 pound raw large shrimp, tails on

3 tablespoons chili powder

1 teaspoon cumin

¼ teaspoon sea salt

⅛ teaspoon cayenne pepper

Avocado oil in an oil mister

SPECIAL TOOLS:

 BLENDER

MANGO GAZPACHO
AND BLACKENED SHRIMP
• • • SHOOTERS • • •

 SERVES: 4-6   PREP TIME: 20 MIN.   🔥 COOK TIME: 12 MIN.

These Blackened Shrimp will heat up a hot summer party, but the cool Mango Gazpacho will put out the fire. The soup perfectly combines spicy jalapeño peppers, sweet mango, and cool cucumber in a complex dish. What's more, everyone gets the fun of doing shots together!

1. In a blender, blend the mangoes, orange juice, lime juice, garlic, and jalapeño peppers on high until completely smooth. Add the bell pepper, cucumber, green onions, and cilantro, and pulse until blended. Avoid puréeing the mixture because you want to preserve the texture and color of these last ingredients. Place the soup in the refrigerator to chill.

2. Preheat the oven to 400°F.

3. Peel and devein the shrimp, leaving the tails on. Pat them dry, and transfer them to a plastic bag. Add the chili powder, cumin, sea salt, and cayenne pepper to the bag, and toss the shrimp until well coated.

4. Spray a baking sheet with avocado oil. Spread the shrimp evenly in a single layer on the sheet. Bake for 5-7 minutes or until the shrimp are cooked through. Remove the shrimp, and let them cool for a few minutes.

5. To assemble the shooters, pour the Mango Gazpacho into shot glasses. Put a large toothpick through each shrimp, and place one on top of each shot glass.

TIPS

If you prefer, serve the gazpacho in bowls as a starter or an entrée with the shrimp on top.

SEARED TUNA WITH
• • • WASABI SLAW • • •

 SERVES: 4 PREP TIME: 20 MIN. COOK TIME: 2 MIN.

INGREDIENTS:

SEARED TUNA

1 teaspoon paprika

1 teaspoon garlic powder

½ teaspoon cayenne pepper

¼ teaspoon onion powder

¼ teaspoon dried thyme

¼ teaspoon dried oregano

⅛ teaspoon sea salt

1 large sushi-grade ahi tuna steak

WASABI SLAW

4 teaspoons Paleo Mayonnaise (page 267)

4 teaspoons coconut aminos

2 teaspoons rice vinegar

1 teaspoon wasabi paste

1 cup finely chopped coleslaw

This Asian-inspired ahi tuna is a treat for seafood lovers. Topped with Wasabi Slaw, this dish mimics sushi, but without the labor-intensive preparation process.

1. In a small bowl, mix together the paprika, garlic powder, cayenne pepper, onion powder, thyme, oregano, and sea salt.

2. Heat a frying pan over high heat. Pat the tuna steak dry, and rub the spice mixture over it, coating it completely. Sear the tuna for 1 minute per side. Then remove it, cut it into thin slices, and set it aside.

3. In a bowl, whisk together the Paleo Mayonnaise, coconut aminos, rice vinegar, and wasabi paste. Add half of the wasabi dressing to the coleslaw, and toss.

4. Arrange the tuna slices on a serving platter. Distribute the slaw down the center of the tuna, and drizzle it with the remaining wasabi dressing.

TIPS

Be sure to make the tuna the same day you buy it. The middle will be raw, so it must be very fresh.

SHRIMP AND SCALLOP
• • • CEVICHE • • •

 SERVES: 4   ⏰ PREP TIME: 20 MIN.

This light and zesty seafood salad is just the dish to refresh you on a hot summer day. The citrus marinade pairs well with margaritas! No oven is needed for this recipe, so your house will stay cool, too.

1. Drain any excess liquid from the scallops and shrimp.

2. In a large bowl, combine the lime juice, orange juice, jalapeño peppers, red onion, tomatoes, cilantro, sea salt, and pepper. Add the shrimp and scallops, and lightly toss the ingredients to combine them. Add a dash of hot sauce, if desired.

3. Scoop the mixture into 4 martini glasses. Garnish with the sliced avocado, and serve chilled.

INGREDIENTS:

1 pound small scallops

1 pound small shrimp

Juice of 2 limes

Juice of 1 orange

2 jalapeño peppers, seeded and minced

½ red onion, diced

1 cup diced Roma tomatoes

4 tablespoons minced cilantro

½ teaspoon sea salt

½ teaspoon black pepper

Dash hot sauce (optional)

1 avocado, sliced

SMALL PLATES

144

► TIPS ◄

If you prefer, serve this dish with sweet potato chips that can be used to scoop up the ceviche.

GARLIC
• • • CLAMS • • •

INGREDIENTS:

3 pounds fresh clams

1 tablespoon olive oil

5 cloves garlic, minced

¾ cup white wine

⅓ cup chopped fresh parsley

 SERVES: 6   PREP TIME: 5 MIN.   ♨ COOK TIME: 16 MIN.

This is one of the easiest recipes in this cookbook. Don't let the simplicity of the dish fool you, though! The garlic and wine add a lively flavor to the succulent clams, and the shells enhance the presentation.

1. Wash the clams thoroughly.

2. In a large pot over medium-high heat, add the olive oil and garlic. Cook the garlic for 2 minutes. Add the wine, and boil the mixture for 5 minutes. Add the clams, cover the pot, and reduce the heat to medium. Steam them for 10 minutes or until the clams open.

3. When the claims have opened, place them in a shallow serving dish, sprinkle them with parsley, and serve.

TIPS

If some clams don't open, you can continue to steam them after removing the clams that did open. If they still do not open, discard them, as they may be bad.

SMALL PLATES

146

PORK SAUCERS

• • • WITH PEAR COMPOTE • • •

PORK SAUCERS

2 pounds pork tenderloin

2 tablespoons dried rosemary, chopped

1 teaspoon garlic powder

½ teaspoon sea salt

½ teaspoon black pepper

PEAR COMPOTE

2 pears, diced

3 shallots, minced

2 tablespoons minced fresh thyme

3 tablespoons balsamic vinegar

1 teaspoon honey

 SERVES: 6   PREP TIME: 15 MIN.   COOK TIME: 50 MIN.

In this dish, rounds of pork act like baguette slices for the Pear Compote. The pork is well seasoned with a rosemary rub, offering a savory base to complement the sweet compote.

1. Preheat the oven to 450°F.

2. Rub the pork tenderloin with the rosemary, garlic powder, sea salt, and pepper.

3. On the stovetop, heat a large oven-safe frying pan on medium-high heat. Add the pork, and sear it for 3 minutes per side. Cover the pan with foil, and place it in the oven. Cook the pork for 30-40 minutes or until the internal temperature reaches 145°F. Remove the pork from the oven, and let it cool.

4. To make the Pear Compote, sauté the pears and shallots in a frying pan over medium heat for 5 minutes or until the pears soften slightly. Add the thyme, balsamic vinegar, and honey, and sauté the mixture for 3 more minutes.

5. Slice the pork into ½-inch rounds. Top each round with a spoonful of compote, and serve immediately.

INGREDIENTS:

PARSNIP CAKES

2 large parsnips, peeled and cubed

3 green onions, minced

1 teaspoon garlic powder

½ teaspoon sea salt

½ teaspoon black pepper

1 teaspoon ghee

⅛ cup blanched almond flour

4 tablespoons coconut oil

4 ounces prosciutto

GARLIC AVOCADO SAUCE

1 large avocado

1 teaspoon freshly squeezed lemon juice

2 teaspoons apple cider vinegar

½ teaspoon honey

¼ cup water

2 cloves garlic

1 green onion

SPECIAL TOOLS:

 BLENDER

PARSNIP CAKES
• • • WITH PROSCIUTTO • • •

 SERVES: 6   PREP TIME: 15 MIN. (PLUS 1 HOUR TO REFRIGERATE)   COOK TIME: 25 MIN.

These crispy Parsnip Cakes are topped with a dollop of creamy avocado sauce and a salty curl of prosciutto. The intense flavor of the parsnips dominates the dish, distinguishing it from bland mashed potato patties.

1. Peel and cube the parsnips. Place them in a saucepan, cover them with water, and boil them for 10 minutes. Drain the parsnips.

2. In a medium-sized bowl, mash together the parsnips, green onion, garlic powder, sea salt, pepper, and ghee. Cover the bowl with plastic wrap, and refrigerate it for at least 1 hour.

3. Remove the parsnip mash from the refrigerator, and form it into 1½-inch patties. Dust both sides of each parsnip patty with almond flour.

4. In a frying pan over high heat, heat the coconut oil. Cook the parsnip patties in the hot oil for 2 minutes. Turn them over, and cook them for an additional 2 minutes or until golden brown.

5. To make the Garlic Avocado Sauce, combine the avocado, lemon juice, apple cider vinegar, honey, water, garlic, and green onion in a blender, and blend on high until smooth.

6. Place a dollop of Garlic Avocado Sauce on top of each parsnip cake. Slice the prosciutto, and place a curl of prosciutto on top. Serve immediately.

TIPS

Keep your parsnip cakes small to ensure a crispy exterior. If you would like to experiment, try using turnips instead of parsnips.

PUB GRUB

BAR

Favorites With

& PALEO

TWIST

PUB GRUB

BACON MUSHROOM
• • • SLIDERS • • •

 SERVES: 6-8   PREP TIME: 15 MIN.   🔥 COOK TIME: 15 MIN.

This recipe dresses up a traditional burger with the subtle flavors of garlic, onion, and Worcestershire sauce. Once you top these burgers with crispy bacon and buttery mushrooms, you won't even notice that the bun is missing.

INGREDIENTS:

5 cloves garlic, minced

1 yellow onion, diced

2 pounds grass-fed ground beef

3 tablespoons Worcestershire sauce

⅛ teaspoon sea salt

⅛ teaspoon black pepper

1 egg

8 strips bacon

10 mushrooms, sliced

Avocado oil in an oil mister

1 head butter lettuce

1. Preheat the grill to medium-high.

2. In a large bowl, combine the garlic, onion, ground beef, Worcestershire sauce, sea salt, pepper, and egg. Cover the bowl, and refrigerate it.

3. In a large frying pan over medium-high heat, cook the bacon until it is crisp, and set it aside. Remove the bacon grease from the pan, leaving just enough to coat it.

4. Add the mushrooms to the frying pan, and sauté them for 1-2 minutes or until they are tender.

5. Remove the meat mixture from the refrigerator, and form it into 10-12 3-inch patties, pushing a thumbprint into the center of each patty to help them retain their shape. Spray the grill with avocado oil, and grill the patties for about 3 minutes. Turn them over, and grill them for an additional 2 minutes or until they reach the desired doneness.

6. Lay each cooked patty on a piece of lettuce. Cut the bacon into quarters, and garnish the sliders with bacon and mushrooms.

BEEFED-UP

• • • CHILI • • •

 SERVES: 8-10   **PREP TIME: 20 MIN.**   **COOK TIME: 45 MIN.**

Nothing is better than cozying up to a big bowl of chili. Whether you serve it in a bowl, over hot dogs, or with sweet potato fries, this chili is pure comfort food.

INGREDIENTS:

1½ pounds grass-fed ground beef

½ pound grass-fed steak, cut into ½-inch cubes

4 cloves garlic, minced

1 white onion, chopped

2 jalapeño peppers, seeded and diced (optional for extra spice)

1 habañero pepper, seeded and diced (optional for extra spice)

1 red bell pepper, chopped

1 zucchini, chopped

1 28-ounce can crushed tomatoes, undrained

1 10-ounce can diced tomatoes with chilies, undrained

4 tablespoons chili powder

2 tablespoons cumin

1 teaspoon cayenne pepper

1 teaspoon crushed red pepper

1 teaspoon cinnamon

1. In a large pot, sauté the ground beef and steak, stirring constantly to break up the ground beef, until they are cooked through.

2. Add the garlic, onion, and jalapeño and habañero peppers (if using). Sauté for about 2-3 minutes or until the onion is translucent.

3. Add the bell pepper, zucchini, crushed tomatoes, diced tomatoes with chilies, chili powder, cumin, cayenne pepper, crushed red pepper, and cinnamon. Simmer for 20 minutes, stirring occasionally.

TIPS

Make this dish the day before an event to allow the flavors to combine.

PUB GRUB

CLAM AND CAULIFLOWER
• • • CHOWDER • • •

INGREDIENTS:

2 sweet potatoes, quartered

1 head cauliflower, separated into florets

1 white onion, chopped

½ cup chopped carrot

½ cup chopped celery

4 cloves garlic, minced

1 13.5-ounce can coconut milk

21 ounces chicken broth

1 tablespoon ghee

2 bay leaves

2 tablespoons minced fresh thyme

½ teaspoon sea salt

½ teaspoon black pepper

½ pound bacon

2 6.5-ounce cans clams, undrained

3 green onions, sliced

SPECIAL TOOLS:

IMMERSION BLENDER OR BLENDER

 SERVES: 10-12   PREP TIME: 20 MIN. COOK TIME: 45 MIN.

This creamy chowder is perfect for a cold winter night. The cauliflower and sweet potatoes work well together to create a rich soup that is dairy-free. It isn't too clammy, so it's also pleasing to those who aren't fond of seafood.

1. In a pot of water, boil the sweet potatoes and cauliflower florets for 20 minutes or until they are tender. Drain them, and set the sweet potatoes aside.

2. Return the cauliflower to the pot, and add the onion, carrot, celery, garlic, coconut milk, chicken broth, ghee, bay leaves, thyme, sea salt, and pepper. Bring the mixture to a boil, reduce the heat to medium, and let it simmer for 15 minutes.

3. While the soup is cooking, cut the sweet potatoes into small cubes.

4. In a skillet over medium-high heat, cook the bacon until it is crisp, and then chop it.

5. Transfer the soup in batches along with half of the cubed sweet potatoes to a blender, and blend until smooth. Return the blended soup to the pot, and cook it over medium heat. Stir in the remaining sweet potatoes and clams.

6. Garnish the soup with the chopped bacon and green onions, and serve immediately.

► TIPS ◄

If you prefer a fishier taste, replace ½ cup of the chicken broth with ½ cup clam juice.

You can use an immersion blender instead of a blender. It makes a slightly less blended soup, but it still does the job.

COCONUT SHRIMP WITH

MANGO-HABAÑERO DIPPING SAUCE

INGREDIENTS:

COCONUT SHRIMP

3 eggs

¼ cup water

2 tablespoons coconut flour, sifted

½ teaspoon cayenne pepper

1 cup shredded unsweetened coconut

1½ pounds raw large shrimp, tails on

3 tablespoons coconut oil

MANGO-HABAÑERO DIPPING SAUCE

1 teaspoon coconut oil

2 cloves garlic, minced

¼ red onion, diced

1 habañero pepper, seeded and minced

1 mango, chopped

½ orange, peeled and chopped

3 tablespoons honey

⅛ cup white wine vinegar

¼ cup fresh orange juice

SPECIAL TOOLS:

 BLENDER

 SERVES: 4-6   PREP TIME: 20 MIN.   🔥 COOK TIME: 20 MIN.

These crispy coconut-battered shrimp are sure to satisfy your fried-food cravings. The Mango-Habañero Dipping Sauce adds a sweet and spicy flair, and you can easily convert this appetizer into dinner by serving it with coleslaw or sweet potato fries.

1. In a bowl, whisk together the eggs, water, coconut flour, and cayenne pepper.

2. Place the shredded coconut on a small plate.

3. Peel the raw shrimp, and dip each shrimp in the egg mixture. Then coat the shrimp with the shredded coconut.

4. In a large frying pan, heat the coconut oil on high. Fry the shrimp for 3 minutes. Turn them over, and fry them for an additional 2-3 minutes, being careful not to crowd them. Add additional coconut oil to the pan as necessary to keep the shrimp from sticking. Remove the shrimp when they are golden brown, and place them on a paper towel.

5. To prepare the sauce, melt the coconut oil in a small saucepan. Sauté the garlic, onion, and habañero pepper in the oil for 3 minutes or until the onion is translucent. Add the mango and orange to the mixture, and cook for an additional 2 minutes.

6. Transfer the contents of the saucepan to a blender, and add the honey, vinegar, and orange juice. Blend until smooth, and serve the sauce with the shrimp.

TIPS

The Mango-Habañero Dipping Sauce can be made ahead of time and refrigerated.

Consider using a large electric skillet, or simply using 2 large frying pans so that you can cook all of the shrimp at once.

PUB GRUB

160

JALAPENO AND BACON
• • • CHICKEN ROLLS • • •

INGREDIENTS:

1 avocado

6 strips bacon, cooked and chopped

⅓ cup minced pickled jalapeño peppers

⅓ cup blanched almond flour

½ teaspoon garlic powder

½ teaspoon onion powder

⅛ teaspoon sea salt

6 chicken breasts

Toothpicks

1 egg

Avocado oil in an oil mister

 SERVES: 6   PREP TIME: 15 MIN.   COOK TIME: 45 MIN.

Looking for a new way to prepare chicken breasts? These crispy "breaded" chicken rolls are stuffed with a decadent, creamy avocado and jalapeño filling.

1. Preheat the oven to 400°F.

2. In a bowl, mash the avocado. Stir in the bacon and jalapeño peppers. Set the mixture aside.

3. In a shallow dish, mix together the almond flour, garlic powder, onion powder, and sea salt.

4. Place the chicken breasts between 2 pieces of plastic wrap, and pound them with a meat mallet or rolling pin until they are ½-inch thick. Remove the plastic wrap, and spread a spoonful of the avocado mixture in the center of each chicken breast, leaving a ½-inch border around the edges. Roll each chicken breasts closed, and secure them with toothpicks.

5. In a shallow dish, beat the egg.

6. Line a baking sheet with foil, and coat it with avocado oil.

7. Roll each stuffed chicken breast in the egg, then the almond flour mixture, and place them on the baking sheet. Bake the chicken for 25 minutes. Then broil it on high for 2-4 more minutes until the tops are brown and crispy.

TIPS

To make this dish an appetizer, let the chicken cool, and cut it into ½-inch rounds.

PUB GRUB

ORANGE-CHIPOTLE
• • • BARBECUE CHICKEN WINGS • • •

INGREDIENTS:
CHICKEN WINGS

2 tablespoons chili powder

1½ teaspoons cumin

1 teaspoon onion powder

1 teaspoon cayenne pepper

Avocado oil in an oil mister

2 pounds chicken drumettes or wings

ORANGE-CHIPOTLE BARBECUE SAUCE

⅓ white onion, diced

2 cloves garlic, minced

2 tablespoons tomato paste

½ cup fresh orange juice

2 tablespoons maple syrup

2-4 chipotle peppers in adobo sauce

SPECIAL TOOLS:

 BLENDER

 SERVES: 6   PREP TIME: 20 MIN.   COOK TIME: 55 MIN.

These chicken wings are coated with a spice rub that is much subtler than what you get on Buffalo wings in bars. Then they're brushed with tangy Orange-Chipotle Barbecue Sauce, which always has my guests raving.

1. Preheat the oven to 400°F.

2. In a bowl, combine the chili powder, cumin, onion powder, and cayenne pepper. Set it aside.

3. Line a baking pan with foil, and spray it with avocado oil. Place the drumettes or wings in the pan, and rub them with the spice mixture, coating both sides. Bake the chicken for 40 minutes.

4. Meanwhile, in a small saucepan over medium-high heat, sauté the onion and garlic. Add the tomato paste, orange juice, maple syrup, and chipotle peppers, and simmer the mixture for 5 minutes.

5. Pour the onion and garlic mixture into a blender, and blend on high until smooth.

6. When the chicken is done, remove it from the oven, and brush it with the barbecue sauce. Bake it for an additional 5-10 minutes. Then broil the chicken on high on the middle rack for 3-5 minutes to make the skin extra crispy. Serve it with extra sauce on the side.

TIPS

You can store the extra Orange-Chipotle Barbecue Sauce in the refrigerator for up to 7 days or freeze it for your next event.

PUB GRUB

164

INGREDIENTS:

4 chicken breasts

2 teaspoons coconut sugar

1 teaspoon chipotle chili powder

1 teaspoon onion powder

1 teaspoon garlic powder

1 teaspoon curry powder

½ teaspoon oregano

½ teaspoon paprika

⅛ teaspoon cayenne pepper

½ pound bacon

Avocado oil in an oil mister

SPECIAL TOOLS:

 WIRE RACK

BACON-WRAPPED

• • • CHICKEN • • •

 SERVES: 4-6   PREP TIME: 10 MIN.   COOK TIME: 30 MIN.

Whether you are hosting a poolside barbecue or just fixing a simple dinner at home, this dish is sure to become one of your regulars. You probably have most, if not all, of the ingredients on hand, and the assembly is a snap.

1. Cut each chicken breast into 4-6 strips. Lay the chicken strips on a platter in a single layer.

2. In a small dish, combine the coconut sugar, chipotle chili powder, onion powder, garlic powder, curry powder, oregano, paprika, and cayenne pepper. Sprinkle the mixture evenly over the chicken.

3. Cut the bacon strips in half lengthwise. If the bacon is extra thick, cut it into thirds lengthwise. Wrap each chicken strip with a piece of bacon in a spiral pattern.

4. Preheat the oven to 450°F. Line a baking sheet with foil, and place a rack on top of the sheet. Spray the rack with avocado oil. Place the chicken on the rack, and bake it for 25-30 minutes, turning it halfway through baking. Then broil it on high for 1-2 minutes to make the bacon extra crispy.

Alternative instructions: If you prefer to grill the chicken, heat the grill to medium-high, and spray it with avocado oil. Place the chicken on the grill, and reduce the heat to medium. Grill it for 2-5 minutes per side. Keep an eye on the grill in case the bacon grease causes flare-ups. You may wish to have a spray bottle of water handy to spritz any flames.

INGREDIENTS:

CHICKEN FINGERS

⅔ cup pork rinds

¼ cup blanched almond flour

1 tablespoon garlic powder

1 teaspoon arrowroot powder

1 teaspoon onion powder

¼ teaspoon cayenne pepper

Avocado oil in an oil mister

2 eggs

4 chicken breasts

HONEY MUSTARD DIPPING SAUCE

½ cup Paleo Mayonnaise (page 267)

2 tablespoons spicy brown mustard

1 tablespoon honey

½ teaspoon horseradish

SPECIAL TOOLS:

 FOOD PROCESSOR

CHICKEN FINGERS
• • • WITH HONEY MUSTARD SAUCE • • •

 SERVES: 4-6   PREP TIME: 12 MIN.   COOK TIME: 30 MIN.

By substituting ground pork rinds for breadcrumbs and a honey mustard dipping sauce for sugar-laden ketchup, you end up with a Paleo dish that closely resembles a diner favorite.

1. Preheat the oven to 450°F.

2. Using a food processor, grind the pork rinds until they are crumbs.

3. In a bowl, combine the ground pork rinds, almond flour, garlic powder, arrowroot powder, onion powder, and cayenne pepper. Set it aside.

4. Line a baking sheet with foil, and spray it with avocado oil.

5. In a separate bowl, beat the eggs.

6. Cut each chicken breast into 4-6 strips. Dip the chicken strips in the egg, then roll them in the pork rind mixture, and place them on the baking sheet. Bake the chicken for 25 minutes, and then broil it on high for another 5-7 minutes until crispy. Watch the chicken carefully to make sure that it doesn't burn while broiling.

7. Meanwhile, make the dipping sauce. In a bowl, stir together the Paleo Mayonnaise, mustard, honey, and horseradish, and serve it with the hot chicken strips.

PUB GRUB

168

ZUCCHINI FRIES WITH
• • • SWEET ONION DIP • • •

INGREDIENTS:

ZUCCHINI FRIES

2 zucchini

2 teaspoons coconut flour

1 egg

1 tablespoon water

¼ cup pork rinds

¼ cup blanched almond flour

¼ teaspoon cayenne pepper

Avocado oil in an oil mister

SWEET ONION DIP

1½ teaspoons ghee

½ sweet onion, diced

2 tablespoons water

1½ tablespoons spicy brown mustard

1 tablespoon apple cider vinegar

2 tablespoons Paleo Mayonnaise (page 267)

1 tablespoon honey

SPECIAL TOOLS:

 FOOD PROCESSOR

 BLENDER

• • •
PUB GRUB
• • •

 SERVES: 2-4   PREP TIME: 15 MIN.   COOK TIME: 25 MIN.

Can you live a Paleo lifestyle and still indulge in French fries? With these zucchini fries, you can! With the creamy, sweet onion dip, they can be enjoyed without guilt. Serve them hot out of the oven for the best texture.

1. Preheat the oven to 425°F.

2. Trim the ends off the zucchini, and cut them into ¼-inch strips. Then cut each strip into ¼-inch fries. Cut the fries in half crosswise.

3. Place the coconut flour in a plastic bag, and toss the zucchini fries with the flour. Set them aside.

4. In a shallow dish, scramble the egg with the water. Set it aside.

5. In a food processor, grind the pork rinds to create crumbs. Set it aside.

6. In a separate dish, combine the ground pork rinds with the almond flour and cayenne pepper. Set it aside.

7. Cover a baking sheet with foil, and coat it with avocado oil. Dip each zucchini fry in the egg. Then coat them with the pork rind and almond flour mixture. Evenly space the fries on the baking sheet, and bake them for 15 minutes. Turn them over, and bake them for an additional 5-10 minutes or until they are crispy and golden brown.

8. Meanwhile, make the Sweet Onion Dip. In a medium-sized frying pan on medium heat, melt the ghee. Add the onion, and sauté it for 5-10 minutes or until it is browned and caramelized.

9. Transfer the sautéed onion to a blender, and add the water, mustard, apple cider vinegar, Paleo Mayonnaise, and honey. Blend the mixture on high until it is almost completely smooth. Serve it as a dip with the hot zucchini fries.

BUFFALO CHICKEN

• • • BITES • • •

INGREDIENTS:

4 chicken breasts

1 egg

½ cup pork rinds

½ cup blanched almond flour

1 teaspoon garlic powder

Avocado oil in an oil mister

½ cup Frank's RedHot Hot Sauce

 SERVES: 4-8 PREP TIME: 10 MIN. COOK TIME: 27 MIN.

If you enjoy Buffalo wings, you will love Buffalo bites! You get the same deep-fried texture and spicy flavor that you've come to expect from Buffalo wings, but these boneless nuggets aren't as messy to eat.

1. Preheat the oven to 425°F.

2. Cut the chicken into 1½-inch cubes, and set it aside.

3. In a shallow dish, beat the egg. Set it aside.

4. In a food processor, finely grind the pork rinds.

5. In a separate dish, mix together the ground pork rinds, almond flour, and garlic powder.

6. Line a baking sheet with foil, and spray it with avocado oil. Dip the chicken cubes in the egg, and then coat them with the pork rind mixture. Place the chicken on the baking sheet, making sure not to overcrowd the cubes.

7. Bake the chicken for 20 minutes. Then broil it on high for 5-7 minutes or until browned and crispy. Serve the wings immediately with Frank's RedHot Hot Sauce for dipping.

SPECIAL TOOLS:

 FOOD PROCESSOR

• • •
PUB GRUB
• • •

172

PULLED PORK WITH

• • • BARBECUE SAUCE • • •

 SERVES: 8   PREP TIME: 25 MIN.   COOK TIME: 5 MIN.

Prepare this dish in a slow cooker, and come home to a wonderful aroma and a scrumptious meal. Your sweet tooth will appreciate the dates in the Barbecue Sauce.

1. To prepare the sauce, coat a large saucepan with avocado oil, and heat it over medium-high heat. Add the onion and garlic to the pan, and sauté them for 2 minutes. Mix in the tomato paste, beef broth, dates, mustard, apple cider vinegar, chili powder, cumin, liquid smoke, and sea salt. Simmer the mixture for 5 minutes.

2. Add the sauce to a blender, and blend it on high until smooth. Transfer the sauce to a container, and set it aside.

3. Place the whole pork loin in the slow cooker with the onion and apple.

4. In a small dish, mix together the apple cider vinegar, mustard, Worcestershire sauce, chili powder, thyme, and 1 cup of the Barbecue Sauce. Pour it over the pork loin, and cook the meat on high for 5 hours.

5. When the pork is done, scoop out any excess liquid. Remove the pork from the slow cooker, and use 2 forks to pull it into strips. Return the pulled pork to the slow cooker, and stir in an additional ½ cup of Barbecue Sauce. Heat the pork and sauce on warm or low until ready to serve. Serve it with extra sauce, if desired.

INGREDIENTS:

BARBECUE SAUCE

Avocado oil in an oil mister

½ yellow onion, chopped

6 cloves garlic, minced

1 6-ounce can tomato paste

2 cups beef broth

4 dates, pitted and diced

2 tablespoons spicy brown mustard

2 tablespoons apple cider vinegar

1 tablespoon chili powder

1 teaspoon cumin

¼ teaspoon liquid smoke

1 teaspoon sea salt

PULLED PORK

2 pounds extra-lean pork loin

½ yellow onion, chopped

½ apple, diced

¼ cup apple cider vinegar

1 tablespoon mustard

1 tablespoon Worcestershire sauce

1 tablespoon chili powder

1 tablespoon dried thyme

SPECIAL TOOLS:

 BLENDER

 SLOW COOKER

• • • PUB GRUB

174

INGREDIENTS:

POPCORN SHRIMP

1 egg

1 teaspoon water

⅓ cup blanched almond flour

⅓ cup pork rinds

1 teaspoon Italian seasoning

¼ teaspoon garlic powder

⅛ teaspoon cayenne pepper

Avocado oil in an oil mister

2 pounds large shrimp, tails on

TARTAR SAUCE

1 tablespoon chopped white onion

2 tablespoons chopped dill pickles

3 tablespoons Paleo Mayonnaise (page 267)

¼ teaspoon honey

½ teaspoon freshly squeezed lemon juice

Dash sea salt

Dash black pepper

SPECIAL TOOLS:

 FOOD PROCESSOR

PUB GRUB

POPCORN SHRIMP

• • • WITH TARTAR SAUCE • • •

SERVES: 4   PREP TIME: 10 MIN.   COOK TIME: 12 MIN.

Once you pop one of these popcorn shrimp into your mouth, it will be impossible to stop! This simple dish is anything but boring. Double your pleasure by dipping these delectable morsels in the tangy homemade Tartar Sauce.

1. Preheat the oven to 450°F.

2. In a shallow dish, beat the egg and water.

3. Grind the pork rinds in a food processor.

4. In a separate shallow dish, stir together the almond flour, ground pork rinds, Italian seasoning, garlic powder, and cayenne pepper.

5. Line a baking sheet with foil, and spray it with avocado oil.

6. Pat the shrimp dry, and dip each shrimp in the egg. Then coat them with the almond flour mixture, and place them on the baking sheet. Bake the shrimp for 7 minutes, turn them over, and bake them for an additional 5 minutes or until they are golden brown and crispy.

7. To make the Tartar Sauce, in a bowl, stir together the onion, pickles, Paleo Mayonnaise, honey, lemon juice, sea salt, and pepper. Chill the sauce, and serve it with the warm shrimp.

PIZZA
• • • SOUP • • •

INGREDIENTS:

1 tablespoon ghee

3 cloves garlic, minced

3 sprigs thyme, minced

1 onion, diced, divided

1 6-ounce can tomato paste

1 28-ounce can whole
tomatoes, undrained

4 cups water

1 pound Italian sausage

½ red bell pepper, chopped

6 mushrooms, chopped

1 14-ounce can beef broth

1 5-ounce package pepperoni

1 2.25-ounce can sliced black
olives

Crushed red pepper

SPECIAL TOOLS:

 BLENDER

 SERVES: 6   **PREP TIME: 25 MIN.**   **COOK TIME: 40 MIN.**

Have you had trouble finding a Paleo pizza crust that you truly enjoy? Why bother with a crust at all? Instead, try this recipe that takes all of your favorite pizza toppings and combines them into a hearty soup.

1. In a large pot, melt the ghee over medium-high heat. Add the garlic, thyme, and half of the onion. Sauté for 3-5 minutes or until the onion is translucent.

2. Add the tomato paste, canned tomatoes, and water. Bring the mixture to a boil, reduce the heat, and simmer for 20 minutes.

3. Put the tomato mixture into a blender in 2 batches. Blend each batch until the liquid is completely smooth.

4. In a frying pan over medium-high heat, cook the Italian sausage, continuously breaking it apart with a spatula while it cooks.

5. In a separate large pot, sauté the bell pepper, remaining onion, and mushrooms over medium-high heat for 5 minutes. Stir in the beef broth, tomato mixture, and Italian sausage, and simmer the soup until ready to serve.

6. Meanwhile, halve the pepperoni. In a small frying pan over medium-high heat, brown the pepperoni.

7. To assemble the soup, ladle it into individual bowls, and top each bowl with the browned pepperoni, a few olives, and crushed red pepper.

PUB GRUB

CALIFORNIA BURRITO
• • • BOWL • • •

INGREDIENTS:

2 medium sweet potatoes

1 tablespoon olive oil

1 tablespoon chili powder

1½ teaspoons cumin

¼ teaspoon cayenne pepper

¼ teaspoon arrowroot powder

¼ teaspoon turmeric

Avocado oil in an oil mister

1 pound chorizo turkey sausage

1 avocado

¼ teaspoon freshly squeezed lime juice

½ white onion, diced

3 tomatoes, diced

2 tablespoons chopped cilantro

¼ cup pickled jalapeño peppers

½ cup taco sauce (optional)

 SERVES: 2-4

 PREP TIME: 20 MIN.
(PLUS 1 HOUR TO SOAK THE FRIES)

COOK TIME: 30 MIN.

If you aren't familiar with a California burrito, it's a normal burrito that contains French fries rather than rice. This over-the-top dish is deliciously sinful. By ditching the flour tortilla, you'll be able to "Paleo-fy" the burrito into a healthy meal!

1. Preheat the oven to 450°F.

2. Peel the sweet potatoes, and cut them into ¼-inch fries. Soak the fries in a large bowl of water for 1 hour to remove some of the starch.

3. Drain the fries, and pat them dry with a paper towel.

4. In a large bowl, toss the fries with the olive oil, chili powder, cumin, cayenne pepper, arrowroot powder, and turmeric.

5. Line 2 baking sheets with foil, and spray them with avocado oil. Spread out the fries in a single layer on the baking sheets, making sure not to overcrowd them. Bake for 20 minutes, turn them over, and bake them for an additional 10 minutes or until browned.

6. Meanwhile, in a large frying pan over medium-high heat, cook the sausage for 7-10 minutes, crumbling it with a spatula as it cooks.

7. In a bowl, mash the avocado. Add the lime juice, and mix them together.

8. When the fries are done, transfer them to a plate. Top them with the sausage, onion, tomato, cilantro, avocado, and jalapeño peppers. If desired, drizzle taco sauce on top.

PUB GRUB

180

SALOON
SIDES

Tasty SIDE DISHES TO *Complete Your* PLATE

SALOON SIDES

PARSNIP

• • • CHIPS • • •

INGREDIENTS:

2 large parsnips

1 tablespoon coconut oil

1 tablespoon chili powder

½ teaspoon cumin

½ teaspoon garlic powder

¼ teaspoon cayenne pepper

¼ teaspoon sea salt

Avocado oil in an oil mister

 SERVES: 2-4   **PREP TIME: 5 MIN.**   **COOK TIME: 15-20 MIN.**

Are you looking for an innovative chip candidate? Parsnips get my vote! They are round, mild in flavor, season easily, and crisp wonderfully in the oven.

1. Preheat the oven to 475°F.

2. Peel the parsnips, and cut off the ends. Slice the parsnips into ⅛-inch rounds. A mandoline ensures consistent thickness.

3. In a large bowl, combine the coconut oil, chili powder, cumin, garlic powder, cayenne pepper, and sea salt. Add the parsnip rounds, and toss to coat them.

4. Line 2 baking sheets with foil, and coat them with avocado oil. Spread the parsnips in a single layer on the sheets, making sure that they don't overlap. Bake the parsnips for 10 minutes, turn them over, and bake them for an additional 5-10 minutes or until slightly browned. Keep a close watch to prevent them from burning, and serve them immediately.

SPECIAL TOOLS:

 MANDOLINE

SALOON SIDES

184

►| TIPS |◄

These chips do not store well, so eat them promptly. This won't be a problem since they're irresistible!

INGREDIENTS:

1 large white onion

1 teaspoon coconut flour

¼ cup pork rinds

¼ cup blanched almond flour

½ teaspoon garlic powder

½ teaspoon onion powder

Dash cayenne pepper

1 egg

Avocado oil in an oil mister

SPECIAL TOOLS:

 FOOD PROCESSOR

Saloon Sides

186

ONION
• • • RINGS • • •

 SERVES: 3-4   PREP TIME: 20 MIN.   COOK TIME: 15 MIN.

Crispy, crunchy, sweet, and salty, these baked Onion Rings are a scrumptious substitute for their deep-fried, gluten-covered counterparts. Persevere through this messy preparation process, and you'll agree that they're worth the trouble.

1. Preheat the oven to 450°F.

2. Chop off both ends of the onion, and peel it. Cut it into ¼-inch rounds. Separate the onion slices into rings.

3. Spoon the coconut flour into a plastic bag, and toss the onion rings with the flour to coat them.

4. In a food processor, pulse the pork rinds until they are the consistency of breadcrumbs.

5. In a small bowl, mix the pork rind crumbs with the almond flour, garlic powder, onion powder, and cayenne pepper. Transfer half of the pork rind mixture into a separate bowl.

6. In a shallow dish, beat the egg.

7. Line a baking sheet with foil, and coat it with avocado oil. Dip each onion ring in the egg, then in the pork rind crumbs, and place the rings on the baking sheet. Replace the pork rind mixture with the second bowl when the original crumbs begin to clump. Bake the onion rings for 15-20 minutes or until golden brown and crispy. Serve hot.

HERBED BUTTERNUT
• • • SQUASH FRIES • • •

 SERVES: 2-4   PREP TIME: 12 MIN.    COOK TIME: 30 MIN.

INGREDIENTS:

1 large butternut squash
(preferably with a long neck)

1 teaspoon arrowroot powder

2 tablespoons olive oil

½ teaspoon garlic powder

¼ teaspoon onion powder

½ teaspoon dried thyme

¼ teaspoon dried parsley

¼ teaspoon sea salt

¼ teaspoon black pepper

Squash fries often get a bad rap when compared to the sweet potato version. They can turn out slightly mushy. By coating them in arrowroot powder to absorb excess moisture and baking them on a rack, however, you can get a crisp fry! Plus, these squash fries contain half the carbs of sweet potato fries.

1. Preheat the oven to 450°F.

2. Cut off the stem of the butternut squash, and remove the bulb. Peel the neck, and cut the squash into ⅓-inch spears. Place the spears on a paper towel, and sprinkle them with sea salt. Let them sit for 5-10 minutes to allow the excess moisture to escape. Then pat them dry, and place the spears in a large bowl.

3. Toss the squash spears with the arrowroot powder, olive oil, garlic powder, onion powder, thyme, parsley, sea salt, and pepper.

4. Lay the squash spears on a rack placed on top of a baking sheet, making sure that they do not touch. Bake them for 25-30 minutes or until they are crisp and the edges begin to brown.

SPECIAL TOOLS:

 WIRE RACK

▶ TIPS ◀

If you wish, you can store uncooked squash fries in the refrigerator for up to 2 days and bake them when you please. That way, you avoid soggy leftover fries.

Use the bulb of the squash for soup, or simply roast it cubed.

SALOON SIDES

188

SPICY SWEET
• • • POTATO FRIES • • •

INGREDIENTS:

2 medium sweet potatoes

1 tablespoon olive oil

1 teaspoon chili powder

½ teaspoon cumin

¼ teaspoon turmeric

¼ teaspoon arrowroot powder

¼ teaspoon cayenne pepper

Avocado oil in an oil mister

 SERVES: 2-3   PREP TIME: 25 MIN. (PLUS 1 HOUR TO SOAK)   COOK TIME: 20-30 MIN.

These spicy fries are a perfect post-workout treat. Let this carb load help heal your muscles and satisfy your cravings at the same time! Or, pair them with a burger or chicken strips for a divine dinner.

1. Preheat the oven to 425°F.

2. Peel the sweet potatoes, and cut them into ¼-inch fries.

3. Place the sweet potatoes in a large bowl, cover them with water, and let them soak for 1 hour. This will remove some of the starch and help make the fries crispy.

4. Drain the sweet potatoes, and pat them dry with a paper towel.

5. In a large bowl, toss the fries with the olive oil, chili powder, cumin, turmeric, arrowroot powder, and cayenne pepper.

6. Line a baking sheet with foil, and spray it with avocado oil. Spread the fries in a single layer on the sheet, making sure not to overcrowd them. Bake them for 15 minutes, turn them over, and bake them for an additional 5-10 minutes or until browned.

SALOON SIDES

CHIPOTLE-ROASTED
• • • POTATO SALAD • • •

INGREDIENTS:

SWEET POTATO SALAD

- 2 medium sweet potatoes
- 1 red onion, divided
- 4 cloves garlic, minced
- 2 tablespoons olive oil
- ½ teaspoon chili powder
- ½ teaspoon cumin
- ¼ teaspoon chipotle chili powder
- ¼ teaspoon paprika
- ¼ teaspoon cayenne pepper
- ¼ teaspoon sea salt
- Avocado oil in an oil mister

CHIPOTLE MAYONNAISE DRESSING

- 1 teaspoon apple cider vinegar
- 1 teaspoon mustard
- 2 egg yolks
- ½ cup extra-light olive oil
- 1-3 chipotle chilies in adobo sauce
- ½ jalapeño pepper, seeded
- 1 teaspoon honey
- 1 clove garlic
- 1 tablespoon cilantro

SPECIAL TOOLS:

 BLENDER

 SERVES: 4   PREP TIME: 15 MIN.   COOK TIME: 35 MIN.

If you want to add a little zest to your next backyard barbecue or indoor fiesta, consider making this Paleo version of traditional potato salad. The Chipotle Mayonnaise Dressing adds a kick of spice to this otherwise sweet, creamy dish.

1. Preheat the oven to 400°F.

2. Cut the sweet potatoes and three-quarters of the red onion into ½-inch cubes.

3. In a large bowl, stir together the sweet potatoes, onion, garlic, olive oil, chili powder, cumin, chipotle chili powder, paprika, cayenne pepper, and sea salt.

4. Line a baking pan with foil, and spray it with avocado oil. Spread the sweet potato mixture in the pan in a single layer. Bake it for 25-35 minutes, stirring halfway through. When done, remove the pan, and let the mixture cool.

5. While the sweet potatoes bake, make the dressing. Start by adding the apple cider vinegar, mustard, and egg yolks to a blender. With the blender on its lowest setting, drizzle in the olive oil as slowly as possible. Next, add the chilies (1-3 depending on your desired level of spice), jalapeño pepper, honey, and garlic. Blend on high until almost completely smooth.

6. Transfer the cooled sweet potato and onion mixture to a large bowl. Gradually add as much dressing as you prefer.

7. Finely dice the remaining quarter of the red onion and the cilantro. Add them to the potato salad, and serve.

SALOON SIDES

192

PROSCIUTTO-WRAPPED

ASPARAGUS WITH BALSAMIC GLAZE

INGREDIENTS:

PROSCIUTTO-WRAPPED ASPARAGUS

1 bunch asparagus

1 package prosciutto

1 tablespoon olive oil

⅛ teaspoon black pepper

Avocado oil in an oil mister

BALSAMIC GLAZE

⅓ cup balsamic vinegar

1 tablespoon coconut aminos

1½ teaspoons honey

 SERVES: 4   PREP TIME: 10 MIN.   COOK TIME: 20 MIN.

This side dish is a class act. Wrapping the asparagus in salty prosciutto and drizzling it with the Balsamic Glaze creates an eye-catching taste sensation.

1. Preheat the oven to 400°F.

2. Wash and trim the asparagus, and cut the prosciutto in half lengthwise.

3. In a shallow dish, toss the asparagus in the olive oil and pepper. Then wrap 3 stalks of asparagus tightly with a slice of prosciutto. Repeat with the remaining asparagus and prosciutto.

4. Coat a baking sheet with avocado oil, and place the wrapped asparagus on the sheet. Bake them for 15 minutes.

5. In a small saucepan, stir together the balsamic vinegar, coconut aminos, and honey. Bring the mixture to a boil, and then reduce the heat. Simmer for 15-20 minutes until the liquid reduces by a third.

6. To serve, drizzle the glaze over the asparagus.

INGREDIENTS:

2 cups cauliflower florets

⅓ cup tahini

¼ cup fresh orange juice

¼ cup chopped onion

2 tablespoons rice vinegar

2 teaspoons coconut aminos

1 teaspoon Dijon mustard

½ teaspoon ground cumin

½ teaspoon paprika

¼ teaspoon sea salt

¼ teaspoon ground ginger

¼ teaspoon ground coriander

¼ teaspoon ground turmeric

SPECIAL TOOLS:

  BLENDER OR FOOD PROCESSOR

- - -

SALOON SIDES

- - -

196

ORANGE

 • • • HUMMUS • • •

 SERVES: 6-10   PREP TIME: 10 MIN.   🔥 COOK TIME: 8 MIN.

Hummus is frequently considered an ideal dip. Using cauliflower instead of garbanzo beans for the base creates a hummus that is not only Paleo-friendly but also lower in calories and higher in nutrients. Serve it with one of the chip recipes or with an assortment of fresh vegetables.

1. Steam the cauliflower florets for about 8 minutes or until tender. Thoroughly drain the cauliflower.

2. In a food processor or blender, combine the cauliflower, tahini, orange juice, onion, rice vinegar, coconut aminos, mustard, cumin, paprika, sea salt, ginger, coriander, and turmeric. Purée until smooth.

3. Serve the hummus with sweet potato chips or sliced vegetables like carrots, red bell peppers, broccoli, or cucumbers.

INGREDIENTS:

PLANTAIN CHIPS

2 large green plantains

2 tablespoons olive oil

1½ teaspoons chili powder

½ teaspoon cumin

½ teaspoon cayenne pepper

Parchment paper

GUACAMOLE

2 ripe avocados

¼ cup diced white onion

1 Roma tomato, diced

½ teaspoon freshly squeezed lime juice

1 tablespoon minced cilantro

⅛ teaspoon sea salt

Cayenne pepper to taste

GUACAMOLE AND
• • • PLANTAIN CHIPS • • •

 SERVES: 4-6   PREP TIME: 15 MIN.   COOK TIME: 17 MIN.

Bring this guacamole to any fiesta, and watch it disappear fast! By seasoning the rather bland plantain chips with chili powder, cumin, and cayenne pepper, you end up with a chip that works well with the guacamole.

1. Preheat the oven to 400°F.

2. Peel the plantains, and slice them as thinly as possible.

3. In a large bowl, toss the sliced plantains with olive oil, chili powder, cumin, and cayenne pepper.

4. Line a baking sheet with parchment paper. Spread the plantains in a single layer on the sheet, and bake them for 15-17 minutes or until they are crisp. If some chips bake faster than others, remove them, and continue to bake the rest.

5. Meanwhile, make the guacamole. In a medium-sized bowl, mash the avocados. Stir in the onion, tomato, lime juice, cilantro, and sea salt. Sprinkle in a little cayenne pepper for some kick.

TIPS

If you don't have time to make your own, some specialty stores carry plantain chips already made.

INGREDIENTS:

SWEET POPPY SEED DRESSING

3½ tablespoons Paleo Mayonnaise (page 267)

3 tablespoons white vinegar

1 tablespoon honey

¼ teaspoon poppy seeds

BROCCOLI SLAW

⅓ cup unsweetened dried cranberries

¼ cup bacon bits

4 cups broccoli slaw

BROCCOLI SLAW
WITH SWEET POPPY
• • • SEED DRESSING • • •

 SERVES: 4-6   PREP TIME: 5-15 MIN.

Move over coleslaw, because broccoli slaw is in town! This hearty and flavorful slaw is delicious as well as nutritious. It's loaded with vitamin A and vitamin C. The Sweet Poppy Seed Dressing provides an intriguing contrast to the salty bacon bits and tangy cranberries that top this slaw.

1. In a medium-sized bowl, whisk together the Paleo Mayonnaise, white vinegar, honey, and poppy seeds.

2. In a large bowl, toss together the cranberries, bacon bits, and broccoli slaw. Add as much of the dressing as you like, and serve.

CHICKEN CAESAR
• • • ENDIVE BOATS • • •

INGREDIENTS:

CAESAR DRESSING

1 avocado

½ cup olive oil

3 cloves garlic

⅓ cup water

¼ cup freshly squeezed lemon juice

1-1½ teaspoons anchovy paste

CHICKEN ENDIVE BOATS

2 cups diced cooked chicken breast

½ cup diced Roma tomato

½ cup finely shredded romaine lettuce

6 strips bacon, cooked and chopped

2 heads endive

SPECIAL TOOLS:

 BLENDER

 SERVES: 6   PREP TIME: 10 MIN.

These little endive boats deliver a bite-sized serving of chicken Caesar salad without the need for a fork. If you're looking for a meal, use the tasty dressing on a full-sized salad, and you won't be disappointed.

1. In a blender, combine the avocado, olive oil, garlic, water, lemon juice, and, depending on how fishy you like your Caesar dressing, 1-1½ teaspoons anchovy paste.

2. In a medium-sized bowl, combine the chicken, tomato, romaine lettuce, and bacon. Stir in 3-5 tablespoons of the Caesar dressing.

3. Separate the heads of endive into individual leaves. Fill each endive leaf with the chicken Caesar mixture. Drizzle with extra dressing, if desired.

APPLE
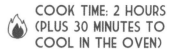

• • • CHIPS • • •

 SERVES: 4   PREP TIME: 10 MIN.   COOK TIME: 2 HOURS (PLUS 30 MINUTES TO COOL IN THE OVEN)

Relish the flavors of fall in these toasty cinnamon apple chips. If you are enjoying a lazy autumn day inside, take time to make a batch. Not only will you have a healthy snack to enjoy, but your entire house will smell like apple pie.

1. Preheat the oven to 225°F.

2. Wash the apples, and cut them in half. Using a mandoline, thinly slice the apples, and remove any seeds.

3. Line 2 baking sheets with parchment paper. Place the apple slices on the sheets without overlapping them.

4. In a small bowl, mix together the cinnamon and coconut sugar. Sprinkle the mixture over the apples.

5. Bake the apples for 1 hour, turn them over, and bake them for another hour. When the timer goes off, turn off the oven, but do not remove the apple chips. Instead, let them cool slowly in the oven.

6. When the apple chips are cool, remove them from the oven, and serve.

INGREDIENTS:

2 large Fuji apples

Parchment paper

½ teaspoon cinnamon

1 teaspoon coconut sugar

SPECIAL TOOLS:

 MANDOLINE

SALOON SIDES

204

CURRIED CAULIFLOWER
• • • WITH MASALA DIP • • •

INGREDIENTS:

CURRIED CAULIFLOWER

1 head cauliflower

1 tablespoon olive oil

1 teaspoon curry powder

¼ teaspoon cayenne pepper

Avocado oil in an oil mister

MASALA DIP

1 tablespoon ghee

2 cloves garlic, minced

½ jalapeño pepper, seeded and minced

1 8-ounce can tomato sauce

1 teaspoon cumin

1 teaspoon paprika

½ teaspoon garam masala

¼ teaspoon ginger

2 tablespoons chopped cilantro

 SERVES: 4-6   PREP TIME: 10 MIN.   COOK TIME: 25 MIN.

The sweet nuttiness of cauliflower emerges when it is roasted, and it pairs nicely with Indian seasonings. Either enjoy the cauliflower by itself, or get an extra kick of spice by dipping it in the Masala Dip.

1. Preheat the oven to 425°F.

2. Remove the stem of the cauliflower, and separate the head into bite-sized florets.

3. In a large bowl, toss the cauliflower florets with the olive oil, curry powder, and cayenne pepper.

4. Line a baking sheet with foil, and spray it with avocado oil. Spread the cauliflower florets evenly on the sheet. Roast the cauliflower for 15 minutes, stir, and roast the cauliflower for an additional 10-15 minutes or until it is browned and tender.

5. Meanwhile, make the dip by melting the ghee in a small saucepan over medium-high heat. Add the garlic and jalapeño pepper to the pan, and sauté for 3 minutes. Pour in the tomato sauce, and stir in the cumin, paprika, garam masala, and ginger. Reduce the heat to low, and simmer the mixture until ready to serve.

6. Transfer the cauliflower to a serving platter along with a bowl of the dip. Sprinkle the cilantro over the entire dish, and serve warm.

SALOON SIDES

SPINACH DIP AND
• • • JICAMA CHIPS • • •

INGREDIENTS:

1 10-ounce package frozen chopped spinach

2 ripe avocados

4 tablespoons Paleo Mayonnaise (page 267)

1½ teaspoon onion powder

¾ teaspoon garlic powder

½ teaspoon salt

¼ teaspoon celery seed

¼ teaspoon cayenne pepper

½ cup canned artichoke hearts, drained and diced

¼ cup diced white onion

½ teaspoon freshly squeezed lemon juice

1 large jicama

 SERVES: 4-8   PREP TIME: 15 MIN.

A party would hardly be complete without spinach dip. In this version, avocados are a nutritious, creamy substitute for the usual dairy ingredients. By replacing chips or bread with refreshing jicama chips, you can savor this Paleo-friendly spinach dip at your next gathering.

1. Defrost the spinach in a microwave-safe dish. Let it cool, and squeeze out the excess liquid.

2. Place the avocados and Paleo Mayonnaise in a food processor, and blend until smooth. Sprinkle the onion powder, garlic powder, salt, celery seed, and cayenne pepper into the food processor. Pulse until the seasoning is completely combined with the liquid ingredients.

3. In a medium-sized bowl, stir together the avocado mixture, spinach, artichoke hearts, onion, and lemon juice.

4. Peel or cut away the skin of the jicama. Slice it into ⅛-inch rounds, and cut the larger rounds in half. Serve them alongside the dip.

SPECIAL TOOLS:

 FOOD PROCESSOR

SALOON SIDES

208

INGREDIENTS:

ZUCCHINI FRITTERS

2 zucchini

¼ teaspoon sea salt

¼ yellow onion, diced

3 cloves garlic, minced

2 eggs

½ cup blanched almond flour

2 tablespoons olive oil

LEMON-DILL AIOLI

½ cup Paleo Mayonnaise (page 267)

1 teaspoon freshly squeezed lemon juice

½ teaspoon dried dill

SPECIAL TOOLS:

 BLENDER

 FOOD PROCESSOR

• • •
SALOON SIDES

210

ZUCCHINI FRITTERS WITH
• • • LEMON-DILL AIOLI • • •

 SERVES: 4-6   PREP TIME: 15 MIN.   COOK TIME: 10 MIN.

This is an elegant way to prepare zucchini. So abandon the salad tonight, and try a warm, satisfying side of zucchini fritters instead.

1. Using a food processor or grater, shred the zucchini. Line a strainer with a paper towel, and place the zucchini in it. Sprinkle the zucchini with sea salt, and let it sit for at least 10 minutes. Use additional paper towels to squeeze out all of the excess liquid.

2. In a large bowl, stir together the zucchini, onion, garlic, eggs, and almond flour. Form the mixture into ½-inch patties, and set them aside.

3. In a large frying pan, heat the olive oil over medium-high heat. Add the zucchini patties to the pan, and fry them for 5 minutes. Turn them over, and fry them for another 3-5 minutes, or until crispy and brown. Cook the patties in batches if necessary.

4. In a small bowl, make the aioli by stirring together the Paleo Mayonnaise, lemon juice, and ¼ teaspoon of the dill.

5. Drizzle the aioli over the zucchini patties, and sprinkle them with the remaining dill. If you prefer, you can serve the aioli on the side.

TIPS

To reheat the patties and keep them crisp, bake them at 400°F for 5 minutes, or broil them in a toaster oven.

CHINESE CHICKEN

• • • SALAD • • •

INGREDIENTS:

SALAD

2 chicken breasts

Sea salt to taste

Black pepper to taste

¼ cup slivered almonds

4 cups thinly shredded cabbage

3 green onions, sliced

½ red bell pepper, sliced

½ carrot, shredded

ASIAN DRESSING

2 tablespoons olive oil

3 tablespoons rice vinegar

2 tablespoons coconut aminos

2 teaspoons coconut sugar or honey

1 teaspoon sesame seed oil

 SERVES: 6-8   PREP TIME: 15 MIN.   COOK TIME: 10 MIN.

Chinese Chicken Salad has always been one of our family staples. My dad is a master when it comes to thinly shredding cabbage! So, when I began eating Paleo, I had to come up with a modified version of our favorite salad. It tastes almost identical to the original recipe but without the volume of sugar and oil.

1. Fillet the chicken breasts, and lightly season them with sea salt and pepper.

2. Heat a large frying pan on medium-high heat. Cook the chicken breasts for 5 minutes per side or until they are no longer pink in the center. Cut the cooked chicken into ½-inch slices.

3. In a separate frying pan over medium-low heat, toast the almonds for 1-2 minutes until they are slightly browned.

4. In a small bowl, make the dressing by mixing together the olive oil, rice vinegar, coconut aminos, coconut sugar or honey, and sesame seed oil.

5. Toss the cabbage with the dressing. Top the salad with the green onions, bell pepper, carrot, toasted almonds, and chicken.

SALOON SIDES

212

INGREDIENTS:

MINI WEDGE SALADS

5 strips bacon

1 head iceberg lettuce

2 Roma tomatoes, diced

¼ red onion, diced

AVOCADO RANCH DRESSING

1 avocado

⅛ cup Paleo Mayonnaise (page 267)

¼ cup water

1 teaspoon white vinegar

1½ tablespoons dried parsley

1 teaspoon dried dill

1 teaspoon garlic powder

1½ teaspoons onion powder

¼ teaspoon dried basil

¼ teaspoon sea salt

¼ teaspoon black pepper

SPECIAL TOOLS:

 BLENDER

- - -

SALOON SIDES

214

MINI WEDGE SALADS WITH
• • • AVOCADO RANCH DRESSING • • •

 SERVES: 6-8   PREP TIME: 15 MIN.   COOK TIME: 6 MIN.

These Mini Wedge Salads pack mega flavor. The creamy Avocado Ranch Dressing is amazing with this salad or any other. You can also dip sweet potato fries in it!

1. In a large frying pan on medium-high heat, cook the bacon until it is crisp.

2. Meanwhile, cut the iceberg lettuce into small wedges, and place the wedges on a platter.

3. Remove the bacon from the pan, and chop it. Sprinkle the lettuce wedges with the bacon, tomatoes, and red onion. Chill until ready to serve.

4. To make the dressing, place the avocado, Paleo Mayonnaise, water, white vinegar, parsley, dill, garlic powder, onion powder, basil, sea salt, and pepper in a blender. Blend on high until smooth. Bear in mind that this is a thick dressing designed to adhere to the salad wedges as guests pick them up.

5. Drizzle the dressing over the mini wedge salads, and serve.

TIPS

If you want a thinner dressing for another purpose, add another ⅛ cup water.

BUTTERNUT SQUASH
• • • SOUFFLÉS • • •

INGREDIENTS:

1 large butternut squash

Avocado oil in an oil mister

½ teaspoon cinnamon

1 teaspoon vanilla extract

⅛ cup maple syrup

Dash sea salt

4 eggs, separated

 SERVES: 6-8  PREP TIME: 15 MIN.  COOK TIME: 1 HOUR 25 MIN.

These soft soufflés are divine; the fluffy texture resembles that of bread pudding. Vanilla extract and maple syrup add a heavenly sweetness.

1. Preheat the oven to 400°F.

2. Cut the butternut squash in half, and remove the seeds.

3. Line a baking sheet with foil, and spray it with avocado oil. Place the butternut squash on the baking sheet, flesh side down, and cut a few slits in the skin with a knife. Bake the squash for 25-35 minutes or until the flesh is tender. Remove the squash from the oven, and let it cool.

4. Reduce the oven temperature to 350°F.

5. In a large bowl, combine the cinnamon, vanilla extract, maple syrup, sea salt, and 4 egg yolks. Reserve the egg whites in a separate mixing bowl. Scoop out the inside of the cooled squash, add it to the cinnamon mixture, and stir well.

6. In a stand mixer, beat the egg whites on high for about 5 minutes or until they are foamy and form stiff peaks. Fold the egg whites into the squash mixture.

7. Spray 6-8 ceramic soufflé dishes with avocado oil. Pour the mixture into them. Bake the soufflés for 50 minutes, and serve them warm.

SPECIAL TOOLS:

 STAND MIXER

SALOON SIDES

216

INGREDIENTS:

2 large artichokes

1 tablespoon freshly squeezed
lemon juice

1 tablespoon olive oil

2 cloves garlic, minced

1 tablespoon minced fresh
parsley

1 tablespoon minced fresh
thyme

⅛ teaspoon sea salt

HERB-INFUSED GRILLED
• • • ARTICHOKES • • •

 SERVES: 4   PREP TIME: 10 MIN.   COOK TIME: 35 MIN.

No need to dip these artichokes in mayonnaise! They are already infused with robust flavor.

1. Place a large pot with 1 inch of water and a steamer basket over high heat.

2. Rinse the artichokes, remove the stems, and trim ½ inch off the top. Place them in the steamer basket, cover, and steam them for 20 minutes. Let them cool until they can be handled easily.

3. Preheat your grill to high.

4. In a small bowl, mix together the lemon juice, olive oil, garlic, parsley, thyme, and sea salt. Cut the artichokes in half and scoop out the fuzzy inner leaves. Brush half of the herb mixture on the outside of the artichokes and between the outer leaves.

5. Place the artichokes cut side down on the grill. Cover and grill for 5-7 minutes. Flip them and brush on the remaining herb mixture. Grill for an additional 5 minutes. Remove the artichokes from the grill and let them cool for a few minutes before serving.

SALOON SIDES
• • •

218

INGREDIENTS:

BUTTERNUT SQUASH ROUNDS

1 long butternut squash

½ teaspoon sea salt, divided

2 tablespoons olive oil

Avocado oil in an oil mister

¼ teaspoon black pepper

SPICY MUSTARD DRESSING

¼ cup apple cider vinegar

¼ cup olive oil

2 cloves garlic, minced

2 tablespoons maple syrup

1 tablespoon spicy brown mustard

1 tablespoon Dijon mustard

ARUGULA SALAD

½ cup unsweetened dried cranberries

½ cup chopped walnuts

1 cup chopped arugula

SPECIAL TOOLS:

 BLENDER

BUTTERNUT SQUASH ROUNDS
• • • WITH ARUGULA SALAD • • •

 SERVES: 4-6   PREP TIME: 20 MIN.   COOK TIME: 40 MIN.

This dish brings a striking splash of fall color to any table. The sweetness of the roasted butternut squash and cranberries nicely contrasts with the crunchiness of the walnuts. The tangy dressing pulls the dish together for a side that will impress any guest.

1. Cut off the ends of the butternut squash, and peel it. Cut off the neck, and slice it into ¼-inch rounds. Cut the bottom of the squash in half, scoop out the seeds, and cut the squash into ½-inch cubes. Arrange the squash rounds in a single layer on paper towels, sprinkle them with ¼ teaspoon salt, and let them stand for 20 minutes.

2. Preheat the oven to 425°F.

3. Blot the excess moisture from the squash rounds. Toss the rounds with the olive oil. Line 2 baking pans with foil, and spray them with avocado oil. Arrange the rounds in a single layer on one pan, and place the cubes on the other. Sprinkle the squash with ¼ teaspoon sea salt and the pepper. Bake for 20 minutes. Turn the rounds, and toss the cubes. Bake them for an additional 15-20 minutes.

4. To prepare the dressing, add the apple cider vinegar, olive oil, garlic, maple syrup, brown mustard, and Dijon mustard to a blender. Blend on high until the ingredients are combined.

5. In a bowl, stir together the cranberries, walnuts, and arugula. Lightly dress the salad with the dressing. Stir in the roasted butternut squash cubes.

6. To serve, place a small mound of the salad mixture on top of each butternut squash round, and drizzle them with extra dressing, if desired.

INGREDIENTS:

4 tablespoons Paleo Mayonnaise (page 267)

2 teaspoons mustard

2 tablespoons apple cider vinegar

1 teaspoon honey

⅛ teaspoon sea salt

⅛ teaspoon black pepper

1 16-ounce bag coleslaw

COLESLAW
• • • WITH CREAMY DRESSING • • •

 SERVES: 6-8   PREP TIME: 15 MIN.

No picnic or barbecue would be complete without a creamy, tangy coleslaw. This slightly sweet slaw will have you salivating! It's a breeze to throw together, and it pairs well with anything from the grill.

1. In a small mixing bowl, whisk together the Paleo Mayonnaise, mustard, apple cider vinegar, honey, sea salt, and pepper.

2. Place the coleslaw in a large serving bowl, and drizzle the dressing over it. Toss, and serve chilled.

SWEET

TREATS

· ·

YUM

Delicious

DESSERTS

SWEET TREATS

INGREDIENTS:

2 ounces semi-sweet baking
  chocolate*

¼ cup almond butter

¼ cup maple syrup

2 large Fuji apples

½ teaspoon freshly squeezed
  lemon juice

⅓ cup chopped walnuts

* Most chocolate contains soy
lecithin as well as dairy. To avoid
these ingredients, a good brand
to use is Enjoy Life.

APPLE
• • • NACHOS • • •

 SERVES: 4    PREP TIME: 10 MIN.   COOK TIME: 5 MIN.

This platter of apples smothered in chocolate, sweet almond butter, and nuts will satisfy any sweet craving. It's also a perfect recipe for a novice baker since it's ready in minutes and requires no special culinary equipment.

1. In a small saucepan, melt the chocolate over low heat, stirring occasionally to prevent it from burning.

2. In a small microwave-safe bowl, combine the almond butter and maple syrup, and microwave it for 10 seconds.

3. Cut the apples into thin slices and toss them in the lemon juice to prevent them from browning. Arrange them on a large plate, and drizzle the melted chocolate and almond butter over them. Sprinkle the chopped walnuts on top, and serve.

SWEET TREATS

226

COOKIE DOUGH
• • • BONBONS • • •

INGREDIENTS:

1½ cups blanched almond flour

3 tablespoons coconut flour, sifted

¼ cup honey

1 teaspoon vanilla extract

2½ tablespoons coconut oil

1 cup mini dark chocolate chips*

Parchment paper

4 ounces semi-sweet baking chocolate

¼ teaspoon sea salt

* Most chocolate contains soy lecithin as well as dairy. To avoid these ingredients, a good brand to use is Enjoy Life.

 SERVES: 4-8

 PREP TIME: 15 MIN. (PLUS AT LEAST 1 HOUR 15 MINUTES TO CHILL)

COOK TIME: 5 MIN.

These blissful bonbons consist of chilled Paleo cookie dough coated in chocolate. Because no egg is used in the recipe, the dough is safe to eat raw. Dig in without guilt!

1. In a large bowl, mix together the almond flour, coconut flour, honey, vanilla extract, and coconut oil. When the ingredients are fully combined, stir in the chocolate chips.

2. Line a dish with parchment paper, and roll the cookie dough mixture into 1-inch balls. Place the balls on the dish, and cover them with plastic wrap. Freeze the balls for at least 1 hour or overnight.

3. Chop the baking chocolate, and place it in a microwave-safe bowl. Microwave it for 20 seconds, stir, and microwave it for another 10 seconds or until the chocolate is completely melted.

4. Roll the frozen cookie dough balls in the melted chocolate until coated. Place the chocolate-coated balls back on the parchment paper, and refrigerate them for 15 minutes before serving.

SWEET TREATS

APPLE

• • • TORTE • • •

INGREDIENTS:

TORTE

¾ cup coconut sugar

1¼ cups blanched almond flour

3 tablespoons coconut oil

1 teaspoon baking powder

1 teaspoon vanilla extract

1 egg

Avocado oil in an oil mister

5 Pippin apples

TOPPING

3 tablespoons coconut sugar

3 tablespoons melted coconut oil

1 teaspoon cinnamon

1 egg

SPECIAL TOOLS:

FOOD PROCESSOR OR MANDOLINE

SWEET TREATS

🍴 SERVES: 10   ⏰ PREP TIME: 20 MIN.   🔥 COOK TIME: 1 HOUR 15 MIN.

Layers of sweet apples top a crunchy almond crust in this versatile recipe. This apple cake is on the lighter side and can be served with any meal. It also travels well if you need to bring a dessert to a picnic or Sunday brunch.

1. Preheat the oven to 350°F.

2. In a food processor, blend the coconut sugar, almond flour, coconut oil, baking powder, vanilla extract, and egg. It should form a dough.

3. Spray a springform pan with avocado oil, and press the dough into the bottom of the pan.

4. Peel, core, and quarter the apples. Slice them with a food processor or a mandoline.

5. Layer the apples on top of the dough in a spiral pattern, repeating until all of the apple slices have been used. Bake the torte for 45 minutes.

6. While the cake bakes, prepare the topping. In a medium-sized bowl, stir together the coconut sugar, melted coconut oil, cinnamon, and egg. When the cake is done, spoon the topping evenly over the top layer of apples. Bake for 30 more minutes or until the top is browned and firm.

ALMOND BUTTER

• • • BARS • • •

 MAKES: 32 BARS   PREP TIME: 15 MIN. (PLUS 1 HOUR TO CHILL)   COOK TIME: 1 MIN.

These decadent bars mimic the flavors of a Reese's Peanut Butter Cup. Since you don't have to bake them, they are ready in a flash and can easily serve a large group.

INGREDIENTS:

½ cup + 2 tablespoons almond butter

½ cup clarified butter or coconut oil

1¼ cups almond flour

1¼ cups coconut sugar

1½ cups chocolate chips*

* Most chocolate contains soy lecithin as well as dairy. To avoid these ingredients, a good brand to use is Enjoy Life.

1. In a medium-sized bowl, stir together ½ cup of the almond butter, clarified butter or coconut oil, almond flour, and coconut sugar until completely combined. Press the mixture evenly into an 8-inch-square baking dish.

2. In a microwave-safe bowl, add the chocolate chips and the remaining 2 tablespoons almond butter. Melt them in the microwave for 10-20 seconds, stir, and repeat until the chips are completely melted.

3. Pour the melted chocolate over the almond butter base in the baking dish, and spread it into a thin layer. Refrigerate for at least 1 hour before serving.

4. Cut into 32 bars, and serve chilled.

PECAN PIE

• • • BARS • • •

MAKES: 24 BARS   PREP TIME: 15 MIN.   COOK TIME: 45 MIN.

Pecan pie is one of my favorite desserts. The rich, sweet, nutty flavor is so luscious that you sometimes need only a bite. By making Pecan Pie Bars rather than a pie, you create an easy-to-share finger food that is sure to be a hit at any gathering.

1. Preheat the oven to 350°F.

2. In a food processor, combine the almond flour, egg, coconut oil, arrowroot powder, and sea salt. Pulse until the dough forms a ball. Press the dough into a 10x15-inch glass casserole dish, and bake it for 15 minutes.

3. Meanwhile, make the filling by adding the dates to the food processor and blending them on high for 1 minute. Add the eggs, maple syrup, and vanilla extract, and process on high until the filling is smooth.

4. Pour the filling mixture over the partially baked crust. Sprinkle the pecans evenly over the top, and bake the bars for another 30 minutes. Let the bars cool before cutting them.

INGREDIENTS:

CRUST

1¾ cups blanched almond flour

1 egg

1 tablespoon coconut oil

½ teaspoon arrowroot powder

¼ teaspoon sea salt

FILLING

8 ounces pitted dates

2 eggs

¼ cup maple syrup

½ teaspoon vanilla extract

1 cup chopped pecans

SPECIAL TOOLS:

 FOOD PROCESSOR

• • •
SWEET TREATS
• • •

234

INGREDIENTS:

CRÊPES

1 green plantain

3 eggs

½ cup water

⅛ cup cocoa powder

1 teaspoon vanilla extract

1 teaspoon honey

Dash sea salt

Avocado oil in an oil mister

TOPPING

½ teaspoon coconut oil

2 cups chopped strawberries

1 tablespoon honey

2 ounces semi-sweet baking chocolate*

*Most chocolate contains soy lecithin as well as dairy. To avoid these ingredients, a good brand to use is Enjoy Life.

SPECIAL TOOLS:

 BLENDER

CHOCOLATE CREPES WITH
... STRAWBERRIES AND ...
CHOCOLATE SAUCE

 SERVES: 8   PREP TIME: 15 MIN.    COOK TIME: 25 MIN.

Strawberries and chocolate are always a winning flavor combination. In this case, they team up to make a decadent topping for a slightly sweet chocolate crêpe. Whether you are serving these crêpes for dessert or having them for breakfast, indulge and enjoy!

1. In a blender, combine the plantain, eggs, water, cocoa powder, vanilla extract, honey, and sea salt. Blend on high until smooth.

2. Heat a large nonstick frying pan on medium-high, and spray it with avocado oil. Pour 3-inch circles of batter into the pan. Cook them until they begin to bubble, about 2-3 minutes. Turn them over, and cook the other sides for 2 minutes. Set the crêpes aside on a platter.

3. To make the topping, melt the coconut oil in a separate frying pan. Add the strawberries and honey, and sauté them over medium heat for 3 minutes or until the strawberries are slightly tender. Top each crêpe with a spoonful of strawberries.

4. In a microwave-safe bowl, microwave the baking chocolate for 20 seconds. Stir, and continue microwaving it in 20-second increments until it is fully melted. Drizzle the chocolate over the crêpes, and serve immediately.

ALMOND COCONUT
• • • ICE CREAM SUNDAES • • •

INGREDIENTS:

VANILLA ICE CREAM

2 13.5-ounce cans full-fat coconut milk

⅓-½ cup honey

1½ tablespoons vanilla extract

SUNDAE TOPPINGS

2 ounces semi-sweet baking chocolate*

¼ cup sliced almonds

½ cup unsweetened coconut flakes

* Most chocolate contains soy lecithin as well as dairy. To avoid these ingredients, a good brand to use is Enjoy Life.

SPECIAL TOOLS:

 BLENDER

 FOOD PROCESSOR

• • •
SWEET TREATS
• • •

238

 SERVES: 6   PREP TIME: 15 MIN. (PLUS TIME TO FREEZE OVERNIGHT)   COOK TIME: 10 MIN.

Chocolate and coconut and almonds, oh my! This blissful sundae is my favorite treat. Coconut milk provides a rich base for the creamy vanilla ice cream. Eat the ice cream by itself, or top it with the perfect trio: rich chocolate, crunchy slivered almonds, and coconut flakes.

1. In a blender, mix together the coconut milk, honey, and vanilla extract.

2. Line a freezer-safe container with plastic wrap. Pour the mixture into the container, cover it, and freeze it overnight.

3. Add half of the frozen mixture to a food processor. Mix it on high until it resembles frozen yogurt, and set it aside in a container. Repeat this process with the other half of the mixture, and add it to the container with the first half. Freeze the ice cream for another 30 minutes before serving.

4. To assemble the sundaes, melt the chocolate in a small saucepan over low heat. Drizzle the melted chocolate on top of each scoop of ice cream, and sprinkle it with coconut flakes and sliced almonds. Serve immediately.

STRAWBERRY-LIME

• • • SORBET • • •

 SERVES: 8

PREP TIME: 10 MIN.
(PLUS 2 HOURS TO FREEZE)

This light, zesty sorbet is the perfect way to cool off your guests during a hot summer party. It's effortless to prepare and refreshing to eat. Allow it to sit out for a few minutes before serving so that it is easy to scoop.

INGREDIENTS:

1 pound frozen strawberries

Juice of 2 limes

½ cup honey

1 cup ice cubes

4 shots tequila (optional)

1. In a high-quality blender or food processor, combine the strawberries, lime juice, honey, and ice cubes. Blend on high until smooth. Pour the mixture into a covered freezer-safe container, and freeze it for 2 hours before serving. If you freeze it overnight, let the sorbet soften for 5 minutes before serving.

2. Top each sorbet serving with half a shot of tequila, if desired.

SPECIAL TOOLS:

  BLENDER OR
FOOD PROCESSOR

SWEET TREATS

240

COCONUT-BAKED BANANAS
• • • AND VANILLA ICE CREAM • • •

INGREDIENTS:

4 bananas

1 teaspoon coconut flour

1 egg

1 teaspoon freshly squeezed lemon juice

1 tablespoon water

Avocado oil in an oil mister

½ cup shredded unsweetened coconut

¼ cup blanched almond flour

3 tablespoons coconut sugar

Vanilla Ice Cream (page 238)

½ cup maple syrup

 SERVES: 8   PREP TIME: 15 MIN.   COOK TIME: 25 MIN.

This baked banana and ice cream dish was inspired by my travels to Thailand. This is my Paleo version of a popular treat that is commonly available in Thai restaurants.

1. Cut the bananas in half vertically and then horizontally, creating 4 pieces from each banana.

2. Spoon the coconut flour into a plastic bag, and toss the bananas with the flour. Set the bag aside.

3. Preheat the oven to 375°F.

4. In a shallow dish, scramble the egg with the lemon juice and water, and set it aside.

5. Line a baking sheet with foil, and spray it with avocado oil.

6. In a separate shallow dish, combine the shredded coconut, almond flour, and coconut sugar. Dip each banana into the egg mixture. Then roll it in the coconut mixture, and place it on the baking sheet. Repeat with the rest of the banana pieces.

7. Bake the coated bananas for 15 minutes. Turn them over, and bake them for another 10 minutes or until golden brown.

8. Serve the bananas hot with a scoop of Vanilla Ice Cream, and drizzle them with maple syrup.

SPECIAL TOOLS:

 FOOD PROCESSOR

SWEET TREATS

242

MILLION-DOLLAR
• • • CHOCOLATE FONDUE • • •

 SERVES: 8   PREP TIME: 10 MIN.   COOK TIME: 10 MIN.

INGREDIENTS:

1 13.5-ounce can full-fat coconut milk

2 ounces semi-sweet baking chocolate*, chopped

½ cup cocoa powder

¼ cup coconut sugar

⅛ cup honey

1 pint strawberries, halved

2 apples, sliced

2 bananas, sliced

1 tablespoon freshly squeezed lemon juice

Toothpicks or skewers

* Most chocolate contains soy lecithin as well as dairy. To avoid these ingredients, a good brand to use is Enjoy Life.

This is one the richest Paleo desserts I've ever had. Dark chocolate and cocoa powder add another layer of decadence to a thick, creamy coconut milk base.

1. In a medium-sized saucepan, heat the coconut milk over medium-high heat. Whisk in the baking chocolate in 3 batches. When the chocolate has melted completely, gradually whisk in the cocoa powder until it reaches the desired consistency. Finally, whisk in the coconut sugar and honey.

2. In a bowl, toss the strawberries, apples, and bananas with the lemon juice to prevent them from browning.

3. Use the toothpicks or skewers to dip the fruit into the warm chocolate fondue.

SWEET TREATS

244

DELECTABLE

DRINKS

Cheers

BOTTOMS

UP

DELECTABLE DRINKS

BLUEBERRY MINT

• • • JULEPS • • •

 SERVES: 4　　PREP TIME: 5 MIN.

This blueberry cocktail is a great source of antioxidants, and the blueberry and mint provide bold flavors for a unique drink. If you don't like bourbon, simply substitute the alcohol of your choosing, or omit the alcohol entirely.

In the bottom of a glass, muddle the mint, blueberries, lemon juice, and honey. Divide the mixture evenly among 4 glasses. Top each with ½ cup soda water and a shot of bourbon or vodka (if using). Add ice cubes, and garnish each glass with a slice of lemon.

TIPS

If you like sweet drinks, add more honey. Keep in mind that honey is essentially sugar, so use it sparingly.

These Mint Juleps are also great with blackberries!

INGREDIENTS:

6 mint leaves, chopped

1 cup blueberries

2 teaspoons freshly squeezed lemon juice

1-3 tablespoon honey

2 cups soda water

6 ounces bourbon or potato vodka (optional)

Ice cubes

4 lemon slices

LIGHT SEA

• • • BREEZES • • •

 SERVES: 4　　PREP TIME: 2 MIN.

This drink is slightly tart, yet surprisingly refreshing. It's best when grapefruit is in season and at its sweetest. If the drink is still too bitter for your taste buds, you can always add a bit more honey.

In a pitcher, mix together the cranberry juice, grapefruit juice, honey (if using), and vodka (if using). Serve over ice, and top with a splash of club soda and a slice of grapefruit.

*Cranberry juice can be loaded with sugar or artificial sweeteners. As always, read the ingredient label carefully. Look for key words like natural, 100% pure, or no sugar added. You can also use POM Pomegranate Cranberry juice. It is found in the refrigerated section of the grocery store and contains no added sugar, preservatives, or colors.

INGREDIENTS:

1 cup fresh cranberry juice* or POM Pomegranate Cranberry juice

4 ounces freshly squeezed grapefruit juice

1 tablespoon honey (optional)

6 ounces potato vodka (optional)

Ice cubes

½ cup club soda

1 grapefruit, sliced

DRINKS

248

POM-Y TEQUILA
• • • SUNRISES • • •

 SERVES: 4   PREP TIME: 5 MIN.

In this recipe, POM Pomegranate Cranberry juice replaces the syrupy grenadine found in a typical Tequila Sunrise. Grenadine was originally prepared with pomegranate juice, sugar, and water, but bottled grenadine now contains high-fructose corn syrup and other artificial ingredients.

Mix together the pomegranate juice, tequila (if using), and coconut sugar. Pour it into 4 glasses. Using a spoon, pour the orange juice gently over the surface of the pomegranate juice to avoid breaking the surface. Gently top each drink with ¼ cup club soda and ice cubes.

INGREDIENTS:

1 cup POM Pomegranate Cranberry juice

6 ounces tequila (optional)

2 teaspoons coconut sugar

Juice of 4 oranges

1 cup club soda

Ice cubes

INGREDIENTS:

12 mint leaves, torn

4 limes

2-4 tablespoons honey

2 inches cucumber, sliced into ¼-inch rounds

1 cup ice cubes

1 cup club soda

6 ounces rum or potato vodka (optional)

4 mint leaves (for garnish)

4 cucumber slices (for garnish)

SPECIAL TOOLS:

 BLENDER

INGREDIENTS:

2 cups frozen organic strawberries (or fresh)

2 cups ice cubes

Juice of 1 lime

¼ cup fresh orange juice

⅓ cup honey

8 ounces rum or potato vodka (optional)

¼ cup water

1 fresh strawberry (for garnish)

SPECIAL TOOLS:

 BLENDER

CUCUMBER
• • • MOJITOS • • •

 SERVES: 4   PREP TIME: 5 MIN.

This drink will make you feel as cool as a cucumber! The refreshing taste of cucumber mixes subtly with the classic Mojito flavors of mint and lime. Enjoy these poolside or at a barbecue.

Blender Method

Juice the limes. In a blender, add the mint leaves, lime juice, honey, cucumber, ice cubes, club soda, and rum or vodka (if using). Blend on high until the ingredients are completely combined. Serve immediately, and garnish with a slice of cucumber and a mint leaf.

Traditional Method

Juice 2 limes, and divide the juice among 4 glasses. Slice the remaining 2 limes into wedges, and add them to the glasses. Place 3 mint leaves and 1 tablespoon honey in each glass. Muddle the mixture with a spoon. Place 2 cucumber slices in each glass, and fill the glasses with ice cubes. Pour in the rum or vodka, and top each glass with club soda. Stir, and garnish with a slice of cucumber and a mint leaf.

STRAWBERRY
• • • DAIQUIRIS • • •

 SERVES: 4-6   PREP TIME: 5 MIN.

As a kid, ordering a virgin Strawberry Daiquiri was a treat. Unfortunately, as adults, we are aware that they are loaded with sugar (½ cup of commercial daiquiri mix may contain up to 33 grams of sugar!). Instead, try this all-natural strawberry daiquiri that should satisfy your sweet tooth.

In a blender, add the strawberries, ice cubes, lime juice, orange juice, honey, and rum or vodka (if using). Blend the mixture on high until smooth. If the blending proves difficult, add an additional ¼ cup water. Serve immediately, and garnish with fresh strawberry slices.

PINA

• • • COLADAS • • •

 SERVES: 4   🕐 PREP TIME: 5 MIN.

The only things missing from this Piña Colada recipe are the artificial ingredients. Even the fat found in the coconut milk is healthy! So enjoy this blissful drink that perfectly blends creamy coconut milk and sweet pineapple.

In a blender, add the cubed pineapple, coconut milk, honey (if using), ice cubes, and rum or vodka (if using). Blend on high until smooth. Pour the mixture into glasses, and garnish with slices of pineapple.

INGREDIENTS:

1 cup cubed fresh pineapple

1 cup light coconut milk

¼ cup honey (optional)

1½ cups ice cubes

6 ounces rum or potato vodka (optional)

Pineapple slices (for garnish)

SPECIAL TOOLS:

 BLENDER

• • •

DRINKS

• • •

251

CREAMY

• • • COFFEE • • •

 SERVES: 4 PREP TIME: 10 MIN.

Rather than buying a mocha at your local coffee shop, try making this version at home. By blending coffee with coconut milk and cocoa power, you get a creamy texture and a hint of chocolate. With or without alcohol, you will want to snuggle up with this drink.

In a blender, add the coffee, coconut milk, vanilla extract, cocoa powder, honey, and rum (if using). Blend the mixture on high for 1 minute, and serve.

►◄ TIPS ►◄

You can simply stir these ingredients to combine them, but the coconut milk separates from the coffee easily so use a blender for best results.

PEPPERMINT CHOCOLATE
• • • DREAM • • •

 SERVES: 2 PREP TIME: 2 MIN. COOK TIME: 10 MIN.

Creamy coconut milk and rich dark chocolate meld together in this decadent, thick hot chocolate. With just a splash of peppermint, the taste reminds me of a Thin Mint Girl Scout cookie. Add alcohol, or skip it. Either way, it's a great cure for the wintertime blues.

1. In a medium-sized saucepan, heat the coconut milk and water. Whisk in the cocoa powder, vanilla extract, honey, and baking chocolate. Continue whisking until the chocolate is completely melted. Stir in the peppermint extract.

2. Pour the cocoa into 2 mugs. Stir a shot of vodka (if using) into each mug, and serve.

* Most chocolate contains soy lecithin as well as dairy. To avoid these ingredients, a good brand to use is Enjoy Life.

SPIKED APPLE
• • • CIDER • • •

 SERVES: 4-6   PREP TIME: 15 MIN.   COOK TIME: 3 HRS.

This fresh apple cider tastes like warm apple pie in a glass. Savor the taste of cinnamon and allspice in this hot treat. The recipe simmers for several hours, so make it on a rainy day while watching movies or playing board games.

1. Quarter and core the apples.

2. In a large pot, add the apples, coconut sugar, cinnamon, and allspice. Add enough water to cover the apples, plus 4 cups. Boil uncovered on high for 1 hour. Then reduce the heat, and simmer for 2 hours. If at any time the water no longer covers the apples, add an additional ½ cup water at a time.

3. Mash the apples in the remaining liquid. Line a strainer with cheesecloth, and place the strainer over a bowl. Pour the apple mixture into the strainer. Let it stand for 20 minutes until it is cool enough to handle. Then use the cheesecloth to lift the apple mixture from the strainer, and squeeze any extra juice from the apples into the bowl.

4. Add 1 cup of the mashed apples and all of the juice to a blender. Add 1 cup hot water, and blend until smooth.

5. Pour the cider and a shot of rum (if using) into each glass, stir, and serve.

INGREDIENTS:

10 Gala apples
¼ cup coconut sugar
3 tablespoons cinnamon
1 tablespoon allspice
6-10 cups water
Cheesecloth
6 ounces rum (optional)

SPECIAL TOOLS:

 BLENDER

INGREDIENTS:

2 jalapeño peppers, seeded

1 orange, peeled

1 cup freshly squeezed lime juice

4 cups ice cubes

2-4 tablespoons honey

6 ounces tequila (optional)

SPECIAL TOOLS:

 BLENDER

SPICY JALAPENO
• • • MARGARITAS • • •

 SERVES: 4   PREP TIME: 5 MIN.

This drink sounds spicier than it is. The jalapeño just adds a subtle bite to the slightly sweet citrus margarita. So try this drink the next time your Paleo palate needs some pizzazz!

In a blender, add the jalapeño peppers, peeled orange, lime juice, ice cubes, honey, and tequila (if using). Blend the mixture on high until completely smooth.

TIPS

If you prefer it sweeter, add more honey. If you want it spicier, add more jalapeños.

INGREDIENTS:

1½ mangoes, peeled and pitted

1 orange, peeled

⅔ cup freshly squeezed lime juice

4 cups ice cubes

¼ cup water

6 ounces tequila (optional)

SPECIAL TOOLS:

 BLENDER

MANGO
• • • MARGARITAS • • •

 SERVES: 4   PREP TIME: 10 MIN.

This creamy margarita tastes amazing! Because the mango is so sweet, there is no need for added honey or coconut sugar in this cocktail. Serve it with plantain chips and guacamole for a fantastic fiesta.

In a blender, add the mangoes, peeled orange, lime juice, ice cubes, water, and tequila (if using). Blend on high until smooth, and serve immediately.

• • •
DRINKS
• • •

254

INGREDIENTS:

1 orange, peeled

1 cup freshly squeezed lime juice

4 cups ice cubes

4 tablespoons coconut sugar

6 ounces tequila (optional)

SPECIAL TOOLS:

 BLENDER

CLASSIC
• • • MARGARITAS • • •

 SERVES: 4   PREP TIME: 5 MIN.

What makes this classic margarita unique is that it contains orange juice instead of triple sec. Say goodbye to the syrupy liquor, and try this lighter version. Blend it up or stir it up. Either way, you will soon be drinking up!

Blended Method

In a blender, add the peeled orange, lime juice, ice cubes, coconut sugar, and tequila (if using). Blend the mixture on high until smooth.

Stirred Method

Juice the orange, and add the orange juice, lime juice, coconut sugar, and tequila to a pitcher. Stir until the sugar is dissolved, and serve over ice.

INGREDIENTS:

1 avocado

1 orange, peeled

1 cup freshly squeezed lime juice

4 tablespoons honey

4 cups ice cubes

6 ounces tequila (optional)

SPECIAL TOOLS:

 BLENDER

CREAMY
• • • AVOCADO-RITA • • •

 SERVES: 4   PREP TIME: 5 MIN.

Don't let the name mislead you; this margarita does not taste like avocado! The avocado just gives it an amazingly creamy consistency and a beautiful green color. Feel good drinking this cocktail, knowing that it is high in healthy fats and antioxidants.

1. Peel and pit the avocado.

2. In a blender, add the avocado, peeled orange, lime juice, honey, ice cubes, and tequila (if using). Blend the mixture on high until completely smooth, and serve immediately.

DRINKS

256

PEACH

 SERVES: 4-6    PREP TIME: 7 MIN.   COOK TIME: 5 MIN.

These sparkling drinks are perfect at a champagne brunch. The peach purée offers a hint of sweetness to offset the bitterness of the champagne. So skip the typical sugary Schnapps traditionally used in Bellinis, and make these instead!

1. Cut 1 peach into ½-inch cubes. In a small saucepan, stir together ¾ cup water and the cubed peach. Boil the mixture over high heat for 5 minutes.

2. Add the mixture to a blender with an additional ⅛ cup water. Blend on high until completely smooth.

3. Add a small spoonful of peach purée to the bottom of each champagne glass. Slice the remaining peach very thinly, and add a small slice of peach to each glass. Pour the chilled champagne over the peach purée, and serve with a stirrer.

INGREDIENTS:

2 pears

¾ cup + ⅛ cup water

1 bottle champagne

SPECIAL TOOLS:

 BLENDER

PEAR

 SERVES: 4-6   PREP TIME: 7 MIN.   COOK TIME: 5 MIN.

Pear is a great fruit to use for Bellinis during fall and winter when peaches aren't in season. The pear lends a subtle flavor to the champagne that is very refreshing!

1. Cut 1 pear into ½-inch cubes. In a small saucepan, stir together ¾ cup water and the cubed pear. Boil the mixture over high heat for 5 minutes.

2. Add the mixture to a blender with an additional ⅛ cup water. Blend on high until completely smooth.

3. Add a small spoonful of pear purée to the bottom of each champagne glass. Slice the remaining pear very thinly, and add a small slice of pear to each glass. Pour chilled champagne on top of the pear purée, and serve with a stirrer.

DRINKS

258

TROPICAL PINEAPPLE

• • • SANGRIA • • •

 SERVES: 6-8   PREP TIME: 15 MIN. (PLUS 1 HOUR TO CHILL)

You're sure to enjoy this sangria made with white wine instead of the traditional red. The fresh fruit flavors permeate the wine. Sip it down, and don't hesitate to eat the fruit as well!

INGREDIENTS:

1 orange

1 lemon

¼ cup coconut sugar

1 bottle white wine

1½ cups cubed fresh pineapple

2 cups soda water

1. Slice the orange and lemon into thin rounds, and remove any visible seeds.

2. In a pitcher, stir together the coconut sugar and white wine until the sugar is dissolved. Add the pineapple, orange, and lemon slices. Refrigerate for 4 hours or until ready to serve.

3. Right before serving, add the soda water.

PERFECT PEAR

• • • SANGRIA • • •

 SERVES: 6-8   PREP TIME: 15 MIN. (PLUS 1 HOUR TO CHILL)

This full-flavored red wine sangria still uses the traditional citrus fruits, but it also adds a sweet pear and a crisp apple to the mix. Serve this distinctive chilled wine on a sunny fall day!

INGREDIENTS:

Juice of 1 lime

Juice of 1 orange

½ orange

1 red apple

1 pear

¼ cup coconut sugar

1 bottle red wine

2 cups soda water

1. Add the lime juice and orange juice to a pitcher.

2. Thinly slice the orange into rounds, removing any visible seeds. Core the apple and pear, and cube them.

3. Add the coconut sugar and red wine to the pitcher, and stir until the sugar is dissolved. Add the sliced orange, apple, and pear. Refrigerate until ready to serve.

4. Pour in the soda water right before serving.

DRINKS

260

CLASSY

• • • COSMOS • • •

 SERVES: 4   PREP TIME: 5 MIN.

INGREDIENTS:

1 cup ice cubes

6 ounces potato vodka

½ cup fresh orange juice

6 ounces fresh cranberry juice* or POM Pomegranate Cranberry Juice

4 teaspoons freshly squeezed lime juice

The Cosmo is the go-to cocktail for many women. In this Paleo rendition, I have replaced Cointreau with fresh orange juice. Like all martinis, these drinks are strong and are best sipped slowly.

Place the ice cubes in a martini shaker. Add the vodka, orange juice, cranberry juice, and lime juice to the shaker. Cover, and shake well. Strain into 4 martini glasses, and serve.

*Cranberry juice can be loaded with sugar or artificial sweeteners. As always, read the ingredient label carefully. Look for key words like natural, 100% pure, or no sugar added. You can also use POM Pomegranate Cranberry juice. It is found in the refrigerated section of your grocery store and contains no added sugar, preservatives, or colors.

DIRTY

• • • MARTINIS • • •

 SERVES: 4   PREP TIME: 5 MIN.

INGREDIENTS:

1 cup ice cubes

6 ounces potato vodka or gin

¼ cup brine from olives

Splash dry vermouth

8 stuffed green olives

The Dirty Martini may appeal to men more than the Cosmo. It is not sweet, but it goes down smoothly. Buy a good-quality vodka or gin because it will greatly affect the taste of this martini.

Add the ice to a martini shaker. Pour in the vodka or gin, olive brine, and vermouth. Cover, and shake well. Pour into 4 chilled martini glasses, and serve with 2 olives per glass.

DRINKS

262

INGREDIENTS:

6 ounces potato vodka

2 cups coconut milk

⅓ cup canned unsweetened pumpkin

⅓ cup honey

½ teaspoon vanilla extract

1 teaspoon pumpkin pie spice

1 cup ice cubes

SPECIAL TOOLS:

 BLENDER

PUMPKIN PIE
• • • MARTINIS • • •

 SERVES: 4   PREP TIME: 5 MIN.

If you can't wait until autumn for pumpkin pie, this pumpkin-tini is just the martini for you! Try it at Halloween while you carve pumpkins or at Thanksgiving while you carve the turkey.

In a blender, add the vodka, coconut milk, pumpkin, honey, vanilla extract, pumpkin pie spice, and ice cubes. Blend the mixture on high until smooth, and pour into glasses.

INGREDIENTS:

8 ounces potato vodka

5 cups cubed seedless watermelon

⅛ cup freshly squeezed lime juice

⅛ cup coconut sugar

2 cups ice cubes

SPECIAL TOOLS:

 BLENDER

WATERMELON
• • • SLUSHI-TINIS • • •

 SERVES: 4   PREP TIME: 5 MIN.

Wondering what to do with leftover watermelon? Serve watermelon-tinis! Watermelon provides a sweet, flavorful base for this mouthwatering cocktail.

In a blender, add the vodka, watermelon, lime juice, coconut sugar, and ice cubes. Blend the mixture on high until smooth, and serve immediately.

CONDIMENTS
& Sauces
A PERFECT
ACCESSORY
FOR ANY FOOD

BACONNAISE

• • • DRESSING • • •

 MAKES: 1 CUP   PREP TIME: 5 MIN.

1. In a blender, combine the egg yolks, apple cider vinegar, honey, and sea salt. Blend on low.

2. In a microwave-safe dish, add the bacon grease and coconut oil. Microwave the mixture for 10 seconds or until it is liquid.

3. Add the olive oil to the grease and coconut oil. With the blender on low, slowly drizzle in the oil mixture very slowly so that emulsification takes place. Continue to add the oil until it is completely combined.

4. Store the Baconnaise in the refrigerator for up to 7 days.

INGREDIENTS:

3 egg yolks

1 teaspoon apple cider vinegar

½ teaspoon honey

½ teaspoon sea salt

⅓ cup bacon grease

½ cup coconut oil

⅛ cup extra-light olive oil

SPECIAL TOOLS:

 BLENDER

PALEO

• • • MAYONNAISE • • •

 MAKES: 1 CUP   PREP TIME: 5 MIN.

1. In a blender, combine the egg yolk, whole egg, apple cider vinegar, mustard, sea salt, and cayenne pepper. With the blender on low, drizzle in the olive oil as slowly as possible so that emulsification takes place. Continue to add the oil until it is completely combined.

2. Store the mayonnaise in the refrigerator for up to 7 days.

INGREDIENTS:

1 egg yolk

1 egg

1½ teaspoons apple cider vinegar

¼ teaspoon mustard

¼ teaspoon sea salt

Dash cayenne pepper

1 cup extra-light olive oil

SPECIAL TOOLS:

 BLENDER

CONDIMENTS AND SAUCES

• • •

267

SAUCE INDEX

In creating the recipes for this book, I came up with more than 20 sauces and condiments. While they complement their own dishes perfectly, they can be used in a variety of different ways. From dips to dressings, these sauces can revitalize your favorite Paleo foods.

Strawberry Syrup	Strawberry-Banana Pancakes with Strawberry Syrup, page 44	Pair with your favorite Paleo pancakes or French toast made from Paleo bread.
Teriyaki Marinade	Teriyaki Beef Skewers, page 60	Marinate any meat in this delicious sauce.
General Tao's Sauce	General Tao's Chicken Wings, page 64	Try this with any stir-fried veggies or meat, or on top of cauliflower rice.
Cranberry Chili Sauce	Mini Dogs with Cranberry Chili Sauce, page 76	Pair with any meat.
Avocado Ranch	Sweet Potato Slices with Avocado Ranch, page 80	Great as a dip for sweet potato or butternut squash fries, or as a dressing on any salad.
Teriyaki Sauce	Teriyaki Meatball Pineapple Skewers, page 90	Try this with stir-fried veggies or meat, or on top of cauliflower rice.
Lemon-Dill Aioli	Smoked Salmon Bites with Lemon-Dill Aioli, page 92	This nice light sauce is great with fish.
Cocktail Sauce	Shrimp Cocktail, page 94	This sauce is great over steamed vegetables like green beans. Or dip crab in it instead of butter.
Pesto Cream	Pesto-Stuffed Tomatoes, page 106	This pesto cream sauce is full of flavor! Use it to baste grilled veggies or for dipping carrots.
Pizza Sauce	Eggplant Pizzas, page 112	Spread this easy sugar-free pizza sauce on any Paleo pizza crust.
Wasabi-Avocado Sauce	Crab Cakes with Wasabi-Avocado Sauce, page 114	This spicy sauce goes nicely with Paleo sushi or sashimi.
Chipotle Aioli	Taco Sliders with Chipotle Aioli, page 116	This delicious spicy aioli is a good dip for fries or a creamy topping for Paleo-style tacos .

Barbecue Sauce	Barbecue Bacon Mini Meatloaves, page 118	Try this with any meat.
Almond Satay Sauce	Lemon Chicken Skewers with Almond Satay Sauce, page 122	Pair this sauce with chicken or stir-fried veggies, or pour it on top of cauliflower rice.
Grape "Hoisin" Sauce	Asian Chicken Lettuce Cups with Grape "Hoisin" Sauce, page 124	Sweet hoisin sauce is great with stir-fry or pork, or on top of cauliflower rice.
Egg-Lemon Sauce	Lamb Dolmas with Egg-Lemon Sauce, page 126	Perfect with Greek meatballs or fish.
Apricot-Balsamic Glaze	Lamb Lollipops with Apricot-Balsamic Glaze, page 130	This sweet and tangy sauce goes nicely with chicken or pork.
Mango-Habanero Dipping Sauce	Coconut Shrimp with Mango-Habañero Dipping Sauce, page 160	This sauce is great with Paleo fish sticks or as a topping on fish tacos.
Orange-Chipotle Barbecue Sauce	Orange-Chipotle Barbecue Chicken Wings, page 164	This sweet and spicy barbecue sauce goes well with any grilled meat.
Honey Mustard Sauce	Chicken Fingers with Honey Mustard Sauce, page 168	Dip lunchmeat or grilled chicken in this creamy mustard sauce.
Sweet Onion Dip	Zucchini Fries with Sweet Onion Dip, page 170	Dip chicken strips or fries in this sweet, thick sauce.
Tartar Sauce	Popcorn Shrimp with Tartar Sauce, page 176	This is a classic sauce to serve with fish. Try it with coconut shrimp.
Sweet Poppy Seed Dressing	Broccoli Slaw with Sweet Poppy Seed Dressing, page 200	Try this delicious dressing on any salad.
Caesar Salad Dressing	Chicken Caesar Endive Boats, page 202	This is a great dressing for a Caesar salad or for dipping chicken.

PARTY
Menus

· · · · · · · · · · · · · · · ·

FOR THE HOSTESS

WITH THE

MOSTESS

PARTY MENUS

Luscious
LUAU
A TROPICAL FEAST

Say aloha to this tropical feast. This summer menu will have your guests doing the hula. It is the perfect combination of foods for a pool or patio party!

SERVES 8-10

Appetizers
Mango Gazpacho and Blackened Shrimp (page 140)
Teriyaki Meatball Pineapple Skewers (page 90)

Entrées
Pulled Pork with Barbecue Sauce (page 174)
Broccoli Slaw with Sweet Poppy Seed Dressing (page 200)

Drink
Piña Coladas (page 250)

Dessert
Almond Coconut Ice Cream Sundaes (page 238)

Preparation Schedule

3 days ahead: Shop for groceries.

2 days ahead: Make the barbecue sauce for the pulled pork and the ice cream for the sundaes.

Day before: Make the mango gazpacho, and chill it overnight. Bake the teriyaki meatballs (but don't assemble them yet), and prepare the pulled pork.

The big day: Make the blackened shrimp, and assemble it with the gazpacho. Reheat the meatballs, and assemble the skewers. Reheat the pulled pork in a slow cooker. Mix the broccoli slaw. Make the piña coladas. Set up the ice cream sundae bar.

Football
FEAST
A MAN-FOOD MENU

This menu definitely scores a touchdown! Serve it at your next poker night or Sunday football party. Many traditional sports bar favorites are included to get your crowd cheering.

 SERVES 8-10

Appetizers
Sweet Potato Slices with Avocado Ranch (page 80)
Buffalo Chicken Bites (page 172)

Entrées
Beefed-up Chili (served with hot dogs) (page 156)
Mini Wedge Salads with Avocado Ranch Dressing (page 214)

Drinks
Hard apple cider
Gluten-free beer
Light Sea Breezes (page 248)

Dessert
Almond Butter Bars (page 232)

Preparation Schedule

3 days ahead: Shop for groceries.

2 days ahead: Make the almond butter bars.

Day before: Make the beefed-up chili and a double batch of the avocado ranch dressing.

The big day: Make the sweet potato slices and buffalo chicken bites. Reheat the chili in a slow cooker. Grill a package of hot dogs to serve with the chili. Assemble the mini wedge salads, and mix a pitcher of light sea breezes.

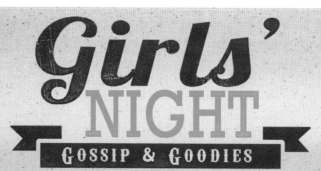

Girls' NIGHT
GOSSIP & GOODIES

Having the girls over for a chick flick? Rather than ranting about work, they'll be raving about the food. Try these recipes to dress up your next bunko night or jewelry party.

 SERVES 6-8

Appetizers
Zucchini Fries with Sweet Onion Dip (page 170)
Bruschetta-Stuffed Mushrooms (page 96)

Entrées
Pizza Soup (page 178)
Prosciutto-Wrapped Asparagus with Balsamic Glaze (page 194)

Drink
Classy Cosmos (page 262)

Dessert
Cookie Dough Bonbons (page 228)

Preparation Schedule

3 days ahead: Shop for groceries.

2 days ahead: Make the cookie dough bonbons.

Day before: Make the pizza soup and the bruschetta-stuffed mushrooms (but don't bake them yet). Make the sweet onion dip.

The big day: Make the zucchini fries. Heat the soup in a slow cooker. Bake the mushrooms and asparagus. Make a pitcher of classy cosmos.

V I P
PARTY
CLASSY COOKING

This decadent spread is worthy of any VIP guest. Filled with many expensive ingredients, this menu should be reserved for very special occasions! Serve it for New Year's Eve, an anniversary, or any fancy affair.

 SERVES 6-8

Appetizers
Crab-Stuffed Mini Portobello Mushrooms (page 134)
Bacon-Wrapped Water Chestnuts (page 86)

Entrées
Lamb Lollipops with Apricot-Balsamic Glaze (page 130)
Chicken Caesar Endive Boats (page 202)

Drink
Peach Bellinis (page 258)

Dessert
Million-Dollar Chocolate Fondue (page 244)

Preparation Schedule

3 days ahead: Shop for groceries.

2 days ahead: Assemble the bacon-wrapped water chestnuts (but don't bake them yet) and the million-dollar chocolate fondue.

Day before: Make the crab-stuffed mini portobello mushrooms (but don't bake them yet), the caesar dressing (page 202), apricot-balsamic glaze, and peach purée for the bellinis.

The big day: Bake the mushrooms and bacon-wrapped water chestnuts. Make the lamb lollipops, and heat the glaze. Assemble the chicken caesar endive boats. Heat the fondue, and cut up the fruit. Make the bellinis.

Fabulous
FIESTA
SPICE UP THE PARTY

This fantastic spread will have you dancing the salsa. These party foods can be served for Cinco de Mayo, Caesar Chavez Day, or whenever you want to enjoy Mexican flavors. This is a creative take on Mexican food with traditional flavors but unique dishes.

SERVES 6-8

Appetizers
Guacamole and Plantain Chips (page 198)
Jalapeño Bacon Poppers (page 68)

Entrées
Taco Sliders with Chipotle Aioli (page 116)
Chipotle-Roasted Potato Salad (page 192)

Drink
Mango Margaritas (page 254)

Dessert
Strawberry-Lime Sorbet (page 240)

Preparation Schedule

3 days ahead: Shop for groceries.

2 days ahead: Make the strawberry-lime sorbet.

Day before: Make the chipotle-roasted sweet potato salad (but don't dress it yet). Make the plantain chips.

The big day: Make the guacamole and jalapeño bacon poppers. Grill the taco sliders. Dress the sweet potato salad, and chill it. Blend the mango margaritas.

Champagne
BRUNCH
MORNING MUNCHIES

This is a fun way to start a day! This menu can be served for Sunday brunch or a baby or bridal shower. It will make it worth waking early on the weekend.

 SERVES 6-8

Appetizers
Prosciutto-Wrapped Melon (page 48)
Avocado-Deviled Eggs (page 50)

Entrée
Sweet Potato Breakfast Sandwiches (page 42)

Drinks
Pear Bellinis (page 258)
Creamy Coffee (page 252)

Dessert
Chocolate Crêpes with Strawberries and Chocolate Sauce (page 236)

Preparation Schedule

2 days ahead: Shop for groceries.

Day before: Make the prosciutto-wrapped melon. Hard-boil the eggs, and make the deviled egg filling (but don't fill the eggs yet). Make the pear purée for the bellinis.

The big day: Fill the deviled eggs. Make the sweet potato breakfast sandwiches, chocolate crêpes with strawberries and chocolate sauce, pear bellinis, and creamy coffee.

Picnic
BARBECUE
BRING THE FUN UNDER THE SUN

This is an excellent menu for a casual outdoor function. With cold appetizers, stirred drinks, and a finger-food dessert, it travels well. Other than needing to grill the chicken before serving, everything else can be prepared in advance.

SERVES 6-8

Appetizers
Spinach Dip and Jicama Chips (page 208)
Marinated Mushrooms (page 102)

Entrées
Bacon-Wrapped Chicken (page 166)
Coleslaw with Creamy Dressing (page 222)

Drink
Blueberry Mint Juleps (page 248)

Dessert
Pecan Pie Bars (page 234)

Preparation Schedule

2 days ahead: Shop for groceries.

Day before: Make the pecan pie bars and marinated mushrooms. Assemble the bacon-wrapped chicken, but don't grill it yet.

The big day: Make the spinach dip, jicama chips, and coleslaw. Mix the blueberry mint juleps. Grill the chicken.

Oriental DINNER

⬥ P A R T Y ⬥

If you miss Chinese takeout, this menu is for you. You may not get a fortune cookie with this homemade dinner, but you can still use your chopsticks.

 SERVES 6–8

Appetizers
General Tao's Chicken Wings (page 64)
Paleo Sushi (page 132)

Entrées
Teriyaki Beef Skewers (page 60)
Chinese Chicken Salad (page 212)

Drink
Cucumber Mojitos (page 250)

Dessert
Coconut-Baked Bananas and Vanilla Ice Cream (page 242)

Preparation Schedule

2 days ahead: Shop for groceries, and make the vanilla ice cream.

Day before: Make the sauce for the chicken wings, and marinate the teriyaki beef.

The big day: Make the Paleo sushi. Bake the chicken wings. Grill the beef skewers and pineapple. Make the Chinese chicken salad. Prepare the coconut-baked bananas, and blend the cucumber mojitos.

279

Fall Game NIGHT

SUNSHINE & SUMMERTIME

Cozy up to this soothing autumn menu. Invite some friends over for games or a movie, and enjoy this warm dinner by the fire.

SERVES 8-10

Appetizers

Mini Dogs with Cranberry Chili Sauce (page 76)
Herbed Butternut Squash Fries (page 188)

Entrées

Clam and Cauliflower Chowder (page 158)
Bacon Brussels Sprout Skewers (page 82)

Drink

Perfect Pear Sangria (page 260)

Dessert

Apple Torte (page 230)

Preparation Schedule

3 days ahead: Shop for groceries.

2 days ahead: Make the apple torte and cranberry chili sauce.

Day before: Make the clam chowder. Prepare the herbed butternut squash fries (but don't bake them yet). Make the perfect pear sangria, and chill.

The big day: Heat the chowder in a slow cooker. Make the bacon Brussels sprout skewers. Heat the mini dogs in the cranberry chili sauce, and bake the herbed butternut squash fries.

Backyard BASH
SUNSHINE & SUMMERTIME

This menu will be a go-to for Memorial Day, Fourth of July, or Labor Day parties. Buy your sparklers, hang your flag, and get ready to celebrate with this star-studded meal.

 SERVES 6-8

Appetizers
Pesto-Stuffed Tomatoes (page 106)
Red, White, and Blueberry Skewers (page 56)

Entrées
Aunt Esther's Famous Ribs (page 120)
Broccoli Slaw with Sweet Poppy Seed Dressing (page 200)
Spicy Sweet Potato Fries (page 190)

Drink
Strawberry Daiquiris (page 250)

Dessert
Apple Nachos (page 226)

Preparation Schedule

2 days ahead: Shop for groceries.

Day before: Make the barbecue sauce for the ribs. Boil and marinate the ribs overnight. Prepare the spicy sweet potato fries (but don't bake them yet).

The big day: Make the pesto-stuffed tomatoes and red, white, and blueberry skewers. Bake the ribs and spicy sweet potato fries. Prepare the broccoli slaw and apple nachos. Blend the strawberry daiquiris.

INGREDIENT INDEX